Could it be?

ROD PARSLEY

RESULTS
PUBLISHING

ISBN: 1-880244-63-2
Copyright © 2001 by Rod Parsley.

Published by:
Results Publishing
P.O. Box 32903
Columbus, Ohio 43232-0903 USA

Contents

II CHRON 34
" 35

II KINGS 23

1. REMEMBER OF PRAYER & WORSHIP
2. REMOVE IDOLS
3. REBUILD HOUSE OF GOD
4. REDISCOVERY OF BIBLE
5. REASSEMBLE PEOPLE OF GOD
6. REVIVE STUDY OF GOD'S WORD
7. REESTABLISH UNITY
8. REMOVE FALSE DOCTRINE
9. RETURN THE BIBLE TO PRIMACY

10. REVITALIZE MAJOR ACTIVITY OF GOV'T OF ATTENDANTS EDUCATION

Foreword

What Time Is It?

Time is a valuable and priceless commodity. Everything we do is based upon the 24 hours allotted to us on an individual day. Agendas, meetings, itineraries, appointments, soccer games, television shows, and our personal devotions are all scheduled to fit into this small space known as time. We create "time lines" for accomplishing projects. Commercials announce that their product is "time tested" because of its long, proven track record. We "time stamp" sensitive mail and documents. Condominiums in hot vacation spots are now marketed as "timeshare" housing. The world's continents, nations and even cities are divided into "time zones" based upon their position relative to the sun. We look to increase our hourly pay by working "time-and-a-half." Our society is constantly looking to "save time" as if we could add even another second to our day.

Webster defines time as "the measured or measurable period during which an action, process, or condition exists or continues."[1] Time is also known as an age, event, season, or rate.

In 1947, a group of scientists tried to define the age in which we were currently living. Nations and people were beginning to rebuild after the end of World War II which culminated with the bombings of Hiroshima and Nagasaki in Japan just two years earlier. Israel stood at the door of prophecy ready to be recognized by the United Nations as a sovereign nation in a little less than a year.

In Chicago, Illinois, however, an atomic scientists' journal entitled, The Bulletin, designed what would become the best known symbol of the Nuclear Age, a clock known simply as the Doomsday Clock. This clock was created to demonstrate the reality of how close the world was to a nuclear explosion.

An editorial in The Bulletin's July 1947 issue, said, "The clock represents the state of mind of those whose closeness to the development of atomic energy does not permit them to forget that their lives and those of their children, the security of their country and the survival of civilization, all hang in the balance as long as the specter of atomic war has not been exorcized."[2]

When the Doomsday clock was first introduced, the hour hand was set at 12 and the minute hand was set at about 7 minutes to the hour. The world, the clock predicted, was in a tragic morass.

Since its prelude, the hands on the clock have been moved a total of 15 times. Sometimes they have been moved closer to midnight to reflect the world in turmoil among nations in conflict. At other times, the clock has been set back.

One such time was in 1991 when the Cold War ended between the former United Soviet Socialist Republic and the United States. The hands were moved to 17 minutes before midnight. The most recent nuclear arms race, however, in 1998 between Pakistan and India once again caused the hands to be moved to 7 minutes until midnight.

But this careful calculation of "doomsday" or the world's end has been underway since the dawning of creation when Adam and Eve were separated from an eternal, holy God by their sin in the Garden of Eden. Since that time, mankind has tried to number their days until the final consummation of life as it is known.

Enoch, a man who "walked with God: and he was not; for God took him" (Genesis 5:24) and seemingly born ahead of his time, prophesied saying, "Behold, the Lord cometh with ten thousands of his saints, to execute judgment upon all, and to convince all that are ungodly among them of all their ungodly deeds which they have ungodly committed, and of all their hard speeches which ungodly sinners have spoken against him" (Jude 14,15).

It was a few minutes to midnight when the Lord awoke my pastor and spiritual father, Dr. Lester Sumrall, to announce, "It is midnight prophetically. I don't want My children to die of hunger."

For six thousand years the Lord has been preparing the world for the soon and imminent return of His Son, Jesus Christ, through His prophets. Today, I believe the urgency and the message is greater than ever before.

At the dawn of the new millennium, our church and our country stand at a crossroad. Birthed in the throes of travail, could it be that our nation and the world have watched while righteousness stood trial in one of the most contested elections in history during the 2000 Presidential Election?

With America so deeply separated along a great moral and spiritual divide, questions arise about our future, our families and our faith.

Are we ready for reform? Could it be that this election at the turn of the century was a coincidence or was there a cause? Did our character suffer a crisis or a climax? After 36 days without a president, was this a power struggle with politics or principalities?

Could it be that this presidential election was but an echo in the earth of what is ensuing in the heavens? Did righteousness tip the scales as good and evil were weighed in a balance? Did demonic forces of confusion and discord stir this rival between the parties and the country? Was the battle in the White House or in God's house?

The new millennium is also a time of new beginnings. With eight closely contested elections reflected in our nation's history and eight revivals recorded during the existence of the Kingdom of Judah before its exile, could it be that God is giving America one last opportunity to rend the heavens and allow His Spirit to be poured out upon the earth before the return of Jesus Christ?

The time appears ripe for signs and wonders to increase in order to point the nation to God. It seems God is setting before us an open door to our community, city, the nation and, ultimately, the nations of the world.

The people are looking for the God of Elijah, but God asks, "Where are my Elijahs?" Like the election, this will be a time in which righteousness prevails, but not without a contest and a fight.

Are we ready for revival? Just as the angel stirred the waters for healing, could it be those waters are being stirred again? (See John 5:4.) God is once again ready to use the prophets and signs and wonders to call the people back to Him.

Could it be that biblical history reveals that we are living in an age when this generation will not only pray for, but also experience possibly the final revival before the end of the age?

Could it be that America is on the precipice, as Leonard Ravenhill termed it, of a culture-shaking revival where the moral climate of our nation is changed and the effect is felt like shock waves around the world?

One thing is for certain: America is on a massive moral and spiritual quest. Could it be that now is the time to capture the moment and not consume it? Could it be that this is our last opportunity to reclaim America and restore her to her original spiritual and moral foundation?

What time is it? I believe God has positioned the body of Christ on the precipice of the greatest revival before the coming of our King of kings and Lord of lords, Jesus Christ. A climactic consummation of this world as we know it is hanging on the edge.

For generations, Americans built a nation with personal sacrifice and self-denial, based on the fear of God and the rule of law. Our moral compasses may have needed adjustment in the past, but we managed to find our way home, even after dark. Only by a return to these principles, in deed as well as word, can we keep from disintegrating what past generations have established.

In a time of social upheaval and moral and cultural chaos, the line between morality and immorality is once again becoming clear. The internal alarm that was once quelled from alerting us to danger is beginning to once again reverberate from deep within our spirits. In the same way, Jesus is standing at the door knocking, attempting to arouse us from our slumber.

As you read the pages of this book, I believe you will discover the elements necessary for the last, greatest revival destined to sweep the earth. With prophetic insight you will delve into the reign of King Josiah and the seven keys he used to turn the hearts of the people and their country back to God in one last sweeping, spiritual national revival. Compared with the days of King Josiah we, as Christians, must once again begin to exercise seven keys to experience this revival in this new millennium:

- Renew Prayer and Worship
- Restore God in Government
- Repair God's House
- Revive the Biblical Principles of Giving
- Rediscover the Word of God
- Return God to Our Educational System
- Rebuild Our Altars

The Lord is calling from His holy habitation for those who will stand up for righteousness and holiness once again. He is looking for a people who will no longer set their prayer time by an egg timer but instead refuse to let go of the horns of the altar until they come out clothed in the glory of the Lord. He is seeking for a remnant people ready to readjust their moral compasses, reestablish themselves in a godless age and return to the God of their fathers.

The "clock" is ticking. Time is running out. It is time to repair the broken down walls of our faith. It is time to reassert ourselves as one nation under God. It is time to restore the basic tenets of the Bible's foundation. It is time to endow our children and all future generations with our inheritance.

PART I

ARE WE READY FOR REFORM?

If to please the people, we offer what we ourselves disapprove,
how can we afterward defend our work?
Let us raise the standard to which the wise
and the honest can repair;
the event is in the Hand of God!

—GEORGE WASHINGTON

A great awakening is under way in America.

—PRESIDENT GEORGE W. BUSH

America is on a massive moral and spiritual quest.

—ROD PARSLEY

Chapter One

Does History Really Repeat Itself?

Just a few decades ago, during the 1960's – an era of "anything goes," – a front cover feature of Time magazine questioned, "Is God Dead?" Today, I question, "Is God Alive and Well?" Indeed He is. For God never stops working even while the saints are sleeping.

Consider a recent Washington Times editorial which stated, "Religion is on the cutting edge. Faith is intellectually chic. Arguments over sacred versus profane, virtue versus vulgar, responsibility versus raunch are in, in, in. Theology may not be as titillating a topic as adultery for public discussion, but it's likely to have a more important influence on public policy."[1]

At the epicenter of this new wave of religion, a revival of morality and purity seems to be emerging among the masses. America and the world at large are no longer satisfied with church as normal. Therefore, there seems to be a seismic shift from soft-peddled religion to an insatiable desire for the divine. In order to understand this transition we must digress in time and take a look at the 8 closest presidential elections in America's history.

ELECTION TIMELINE

In America's short history, there have only been 8 closely contested elections. This is a comparatively small number considering the years of turmoil our young nation has experienced.

The first election in the newly formed union took place in 1796 with John Adams' ascension to the presidency, which was neither automatic nor unanimous. Before attaining this high office, he would have to surface from America's first contested presidential election. Adams won by a mere 3 electoral votes against Thomas Jefferson to become the second president of the United States.

In the fourth election, and second contested election in 1800, John Adams ran against Thomas Jefferson a second time. Both presidential nominees had vice president selections. At this time, the elections for the offices of president and vice president were on separate ballots. They (Jefferson and Burr, the vice president nominee) beat Adams and Pinckney, but found themselves in a tie. The party which nominated Jefferson and Burr mistakenly assigned the same number of electoral votes to both people. Thus, neither of them had the majority of electoral votes. Oddly, the nation switched and supported Burr over the "dangerous" Jefferson.

Because of the closeness of this election, the final decision for president fell to the House of Representatives. They deliberated for 7 days and voted 36 times before Jefferson was elected. In the immediate aftermath of this election, there was a call to amend the constitutional provision, requiring double balloting for president and vice president. This policy has been in effect since its approval in 1803.

The third presidential election to be contested occurred in 1824 when John Quincy Adams, son of John Adams, won this close race with Andrew Jackson. This was the second and last time the House of Representatives decided an election.

In 1876, Samuel Tilden won the popular vote over Rutherford Hayes. However, the electoral vote was too tight in three southern states; one of them was Florida. America was strongly divided. In the end, Hayes was elected.

In 1888, the incumbent democratic President, Grover Cleveland, won the popular vote over republican challenger, Benjamin Harrison. However, he did not win a majority of the electoral votes. Four years later, Cleveland won in a rematch against Harrison.

In 1960, John F. Kennedy only beat Vice President Richard M. Nixon by 100,000 popular votes in this close election. This was simply 1 vote per precinct.

In 1976, Jimmy Carter won by a commanding two million popular votes but the election was close in the Electoral College.

DIMPLED BALLOTS
AND DISENFRANCHISED VOTERS

Not long ago, I had the opportunity to embark upon the new millennium with our first Breakthrough crusade on

Florida's "first coast" in Jacksonville. I believe that this bore prophetic significance to the message God had given me at a time of uncertainty and political and spiritual instability . . . for Jacksonville, Florida was first in history, and first in geography for the new world.

In 1566, the first missionary outreach in the entirety of North America was established for the preaching of the Gospel of our Lord and Savior Jesus Christ. It was there that God chose to launch the first Gospel message to what would later become America. It was by no accident that I found myself there to deliver a fresh word about a new move of God on Florida's first coast.

It was in the state of Florida that the 2000 Presidential Election caused such an outcry among both ends of the political and spiritual spectrum. During the election, there seemed to exude from that state a spirit of confusion and controversy. I even noticed while watching from afar, that the demonic spirit called racism tried to raise its ugly head.

Let me just interject this here. If you want to see racial equality, don't look in the political arena, because you will never find it. But if you look to the church, what you will find is nothing but the crimson red cross of our Canaan King who produces blood-washed saints from every ethnicity, race and creed.

Prior to the year 2000, no presidential election – in all of American history – has ever come down to 300 or fewer votes, and never in history have we gone more than a few hours without knowing the outcome.

This was the eighth closely contested election in America's 225 year history. Could it be the number 8 bears significance at the beginning of this new millennium?

What does the number eight represent? It represents a time of new beginnings. It represents a day when the past is eclipsed by the future. Isaiah 43:18,19 says, "Remember ye not the former things, neither consider the things of old. Behold, I will do a new thing; now it shall spring forth; shall ye not know it? I will even make a way in the wilderness, and rivers in the desert."

In the first actually disputed election that occured in 1800, the nation waited 7 days and 36 votes were cast by Congress before Thomas Jefferson was elected. This time, in 2000, we waited 36 days. Was it by rhyme or reason?

Why were the battle lines drawn so severely and distinctly? Were the forces of wickedness and righteousness being weighed in the balance?

Could it be that God seeks to combine some form of government that is at least sympathetic to the cause of Christ, along with a strong prophetic voice that makes us tremble should we not hear it? Does the past shed light on this telltale turn of events?

From dimpled ballots to disenfranchised voters, a sinister plot seemed to be ensuing from within the ranks of the devil's underworld to divide America and the church. I believe the ultimate goal was to try to paralyze the church for the last great and coming outpouring of God's Spirit upon the nations of the earth. Even today we are still picking up the pieces and trying to overcome the divisive spirit which has tried to infiltrate our ranks within the church.

Each of the previous seven close or disputed elections took place at a pivotal time in the spiritual history of America.

From the Great Awakening to the Jesus Movement, revival has come and gone. The political arena caused each revival's spiritual demise, quenching them in the end.

Does God need or desire the President to be a Christian to bring America back to Him? Is our nation ready for reform? In his acceptance speech, President Bush announced, "We resolve to be, not the party of repose, but the party of reform."

THE WHOLE WORLD IS IN HIS HANDS

The world may rock and reel under the whiplash of demonic designs too insidious for our finite minds to comprehend. God in His sovereignty, notices and deals with everything.

The Psalmist proclaimed, "For the Lord loveth judgment, and forsaketh not his saints; they are preserved for ever: but the seed of the wicked shall be cut off. The righteous shall inherit the land, and dwell therein for ever" (37:28,29).

Daniel prophesied, "World events are under his control. He removes kings and sets others on their thrones. He gives wise men their wisdom, and scholars their intelligence. He reveals profound mysteries beyond man's understanding. He knows all hidden things, for he is light, and darkness is no obstacle to him" (2:21,22 TLB).

God changes the times and seasons. He sets in place and removes kings. With this past presidential election, He is about to send America and the world spinning upon its axis. Like the song says, "He has the whole world in His hands."

The Lord has brought us to a strategic inflection point whereby the forces of darkness that have assaulted our very values must, for one last time, face the onslaught of angelic hosts who stand arrayed to do the saints' bidding. God is reckoning His position in the earth by placing in authority those who will carry out His divine plan.

As the new millennium eclipses the horizon, God is raising up a remnant who are not afraid to confront an evil and perverse generation.

It doesn't matter what political persuasion you hold in high regard – Democrat, Republican, Independent or the like – the importance of your position is based upon whether or not your name is written in the Lamb's Book of Life.

Notice earlier that Daniel went on to say that God gives men wisdom and knowledge and reveals the deep and hidden things. What does this mean? It means there is about to be a breakthrough.

Do you know what a breakthrough is? It is a sudden burst of the advance revelation knowledge of God which propels you through every line of Satan's defense.

That's the reason Jesus asked His disciples the following question:

> When Jesus came into the coasts of Caesarea Philippi, he asked his disciples, saying, Whom do men say that I the Son of man am? And they said, Some say that thou art John the Baptist: some, Elias; and others, Jeremias, or one of the prophets. He saith unto them, But whom say ye that I am?

And Simon Peter answered and said, Thou art the Christ, the Son of the living God. And Jesus answered and said unto him, Blessed art thou, Simon Barjona: for flesh and blood hath not revealed it unto thee, but my Father which is in heaven. And I say also unto thee, That thou art Peter, and upon this rock I will build my church; and the gates of hell shall not prevail against it.

And I will give unto thee the keys of the kingdom of heaven: and whatsoever thou shalt bind on earth shall be bound in heaven: and whatsoever thou shalt loose on earth shall be loosed in heaven (Matthew 16:13-19).

Peter had received a revelation of who Jesus really was. He is the Anointed One who breaks every yoke. Job 33:4 says, "The Spirit of God hath made me, and the breath of the Almighty hath given me life." It is this spirit in man that gives him revelation such as Peter had.

Through His wisdom, God wants to show you and I things that we can't possibly know with our own human intellect. He wants to give us foresight into future events so that we can prepare to be partakers and dispensers of this end-time revival.

THE CURRENT SPIRITUAL CLIMATE

Lesslie Newbigin said, "We are at a point in history comparable to the one occupied by Augustine. ...The classical vision had lost its power over people's minds, and society was disintegrating. ...Alasdair MacIntyre, who invokes the memory of that moment to illuminate our situation, adds, however, that there is one great difference between Augustine's time and ours: then the barbarians were waiting outside the gates, but now they are already in the seats of power."[2]

Former President Clinton personified the potential of this generation. However, in the end, Clinton revealed his disregard for God when, during the week, he brought sexual perversion into the White House and then on Sunday would sit with his wife in God's house!

Billy Graham once said, "We've lost sight of the fact that some things are always right and some things are always wrong. We've lost our reference point. We don't have any moral philosophy to undergird our way of life in this country, and our way of life is in serious jeopardy and serious danger unless something happens. And that something must be a spiritual revival."[3]

THE KING'S HEART IS IN THE LORD'S HANDS

Proverbs 21:1 proclaims, "The king's heart is in the hand of the Lord, as the rivers of water: he turneth it whithersoever he will."

Biblical history bears record that a king's morality or the Christian virtues or lack thereof of a president directly affect God's ability to produce a national revival.

Could it be possible that our newly elected president is the final link in bringing reform to the White House? His first action on his first day as president-elect was to attend a prayer meeting!

Proverbs 29:2 proclaims, "When the righteous are in authority, the people rejoice: but when the wicked beareth rule, the people mourn." Only a cleansing and revival will save America.

A young man recently relayed the story of one of his friends, a young woman, who served on then president-elect George W. Bush's campaign in Austin to Dennis Lake of the Coalition of Churches prison ministry at Prestonwood Baptist Church in Plano, Texas:

> Governor Bush appeared at a thank you banquet for his campaign staff, and was going from table to table to shake hands with the more than 1,000 volunteers. When he stopped to speak to one lady in particular, who indicated she was a Christian, he also began to engage in conversation with her sixteen year-old son. Governor Bush then proceeded to ask the young man if he was a believer, too. The boy responded he didn't think so.

> Governor Bush then asked, "Do you mind if I tell you how I came to know Christ as my Savior?"

> The boy agreed, and Governor Bush pulled up a chair and for 30 minutes shared with him his experience, and led him in the sinner's prayer.

Nothing can compare to the righteous man or woman who serves as a missionary in his arena of influence. Thus, something worth fighting for is being weighed in the balance. Justice and mercy are crying out for one last opportunity in the land of the free and the home of the brave.

GOD'S ANOINTED

The Psalmist said, "For promotion and power come from nowhere on earth, but only from God. He promotes one and deposes another" (Psalm 75:6,7 TLB).

God intends to have a people who will walk completely free from bondage, sickness and disease that they might in turn be scattered upon the earth as firebrands from His altar to set the world ablaze with revival. For example, He will anoint even a pagan king to carry out His sovereign purpose of delivering His people from captivity.

One such illustration is found in Isaiah chapter 45 which says:

Thus saith the Lord to his anointed, to Cyrus, whose right hand I have holden, to subdue nations before him; and I will loose the loins of kings, to open before him the two leaved gates; and the gates shall not be shut; I will go before thee, and make the crooked places straight: I will break in pieces the gates of brass, and cut in sunder the bars of iron: And I will give thee the treasures of darkness, and hidden riches of secret places, that thou mayest know that I, the Lord, which call thee by thy name, am the God of Israel (vv. 1-3).

God was speaking through Isaiah of Cyrus 150 years before he was born. He was the pagan King of Persia. He was never a believer or converted to Judaism. He was by nature a polytheist who believed in many gods. However, Cyrus is the only Gentile king God refers to as "his anointed." He didn't serve Jehovah, yet out of superstition he did not want to go against His chosen people for fear of their God.

The fundamental political principles of the Persian empire was all-absorbing selfishness. But the politics of Cyrus were pervaded by purer motives, and this brought him eternal honor. God took Cyrus by the hand and accomplished great things through him.

Cyrus became king of Anshan (inherited 559 BC). His kingdom was north of Babylon. He attacked two nations in the north (the Persians and the Medes) and became their king. He set up his capital in 550 BC in Persia. He conquered Lydia in 546 BC. The more kingdoms Cyrus conquered, the richer he became.

The next kingdom for him to take was the Babylonian kingdom. He conquered the Babylonian empire the same night that Belshazzar brought the golden goblets from the temple and the handwriting appeared on the wall. (Daniel 5.)

Recently, there was a famous document found called the Cyrus cylinder. When Cyrus conquered the Babylonians he found out the Jews were there and not in their homeland. He became fearful because they were not in their homeland and worshiping in their own temple. Because of this, he thought he would have calamity and his kingdom would be destroyed, so he stopped conquering other nations. He said he had to get this people (the Jews) into their own homeland so their God wouldn't be angry.

There was a kingdom within a kingdom. Because the Israelites did not have their temple, Cyrus believed strife or harm would come to him. He was fearful of God (but not in a repentant way). He saw something unusual in these people – fortitude, nothing would break their spirits, they would never quit.

Every kingdom Cyrus conquered, he destroyed or broke the spirit of the people. However, when he conquered Babylon, where the Jewish people were in captivity, they could not be broken. They had an unusual faith that he had not seen before.

Cyrus, the predicted restorer of Jerusalem, was the man who God anointed to cause Israel to recognize the power of Jehovah, so that His blessings would come down upon the earth.

WE HOLD THE KEY TO A WORLD IN CAPTIVITY

Today, the world is held captive. The walls of modern day Babylon are surrounding them. They try to pray and don't know how. They go to church and all some get is a lot of entertainment but no anointing. They listen to a preacher, and they are still in bondage. But God is about to anoint some fire-baptized, Holy Ghost-filled believers. He doesn't care what they look like or from what station in life they come from. He doesn't even care on what side of the tracks they were born.

They are a people born in bondage. They are living in "Babylon." God is equipping us to deliver them from the chains that bind them. He is about to anoint us with fresh oil. We may be told we can't do it, but it isn't about us. It is about Jesus Christ in us.

In order to understand the hour in which we are living and the hope we have to offer, we must go back in history, before America was a nation and before the Cross of Calvary, to the era of two of God's greatest prophets and the division of the nation of Israel. To learn more about how God wants to propel us forward, read on. The journey is just beginning.

Chapter Two

Who is Listening?

S piritual awareness is one of the greatest deficiencies in today's church. I question whether most are spiritually awake. It is so easy to slumber, especially when there is ease in Zion. Our religion seems effortless, lacking any real need to travail before the Lord in prayer for revival.

Persecution and trials have always made successful conductors to stir us again from our deafened and coma-like states.

WHO IS LISTENING?

The Book of Proverbs proclaims, "My son, attend to my words; incline thine ear unto my sayings. Let them not depart from thine eyes; keep them in the midst of thine heart. For they are life unto those that find them, and health to all their flesh" (4:20-22).

It is time once again to hear what the Lord has to say.

Why? Because it is impossible to hear the word of the Lord when the world is busy lulling the church to sleep by its counterfeit convictions. Without the spiritual insight and fortitude to awaken out of sleep, we lose opportunities for usefulness in God's kingdom. The cemeteries are crowded with those who have died without a cause for which to stand.

Consider the words of King Solomon,

I walked by the field of a certain lazy fellow and saw that it was overgrown with thorns, and covered with weeds; and its walls were broken down. Then, as I looked, I learned this lesson:
> "A little extra sleep,
> A little more slumber,
> A little folding of the hands to rest"

means that poverty will break in upon you suddenly like a robber, and violently like a bandit (Proverbs 24:30-34 TLB).

The Lord's precious promises are for those who will not be found slumbering or sleeping when the clock strikes midnight and God's Spirit is being poured out upon the earth! In order to understand the prophetic hour of this current day, we must first look back through the telescope of time to the ancient kings of Israel and Judah.

THE NORTHERN KINGDOM

Sin and idolatry caused God's chosen people to be split

into two kingdoms. 1 Kings 11:26-33 records,

> And Jeroboam the son of Nebat, an Ephrathite of Zereda, Solomon's servant, whose mother's name was Zeruah, a widow woman, even he lifted up his hand against the king. And this was the cause that he lifted up his hand against the king: Solomon built Millo, and repaired the breaches of the city of David his father. And the man Jeroboam was a mighty man of valour: and Solomon seeing the young man that he was industrious, he made him ruler over all the charge of the house of Joseph.

> And it came to pass at that time when Jeroboam went out of Jerusalem, that the prophet Ahijah the Shilonite found him in the way; and he had clad himself with a new garment; and they two were alone in the field: And Ahijah caught the new garment that was on him, and rent it in twelve pieces: And he said to Jeroboam, Take thee ten pieces: for thus saith the Lord, the God of Israel, Behold, I will rend the kingdom out of the hand of Solomon, and will give ten tribes to thee:

> (But he shall have one tribe for my servant David's sake, and for Jerusalem's sake, the city which I have chosen out of all the tribes of Israel:) Because that they have forsaken me, and have worshipped Ashtoreth the goddess of the Zidonians, Chemosh the god of the Moabites, and Milcom the god of the

children of Ammon, and have not walked in my ways, to do that which is right in mine eyes, and to keep my statutes and my judgments, as did David his father.

After Israel split into 2 kingdoms, Northern and Southern, or Israel and Judah respectively, the Northern Kingdom had 19 kings and all 19 of them were evil.

Jeroboam, the first king of Israel, was originally a soldier and administrator under King Solomon. During Solomon's reign, he led a 'tax reform' movement at Rehoboam's (Judah's first king) coronation. Jeroboam became king of the 10 tribes in the Northern Kingdom. He set the foundation for actions based upon popular opinion. Thus, he caused Israel to sin by erecting golden calves in Dan and Bethel. (See 2 Kings 10:29.)

In a legacy plagued by evil, Israel, or the Northern Kingdom, and her kings constantly did that which was evil in the eyes of the Lord. Through arrogance Nadab ruled. Baasha followed after the gods of his fathers. Elah was a drunkard who was slain by the upcoming king, Zimri. Zimri was not accepted by Israel and was thus burned alive in his house.

From king to king, each went his own way, ultimately down the path of destruction. The book of Proverbs says, "There is a way that seemeth right unto a man, but the end thereof are the ways of death" (16:25). Out of 19 kings there was not one who was found righteous before the Lord.

Unfortunately, this regime was renowned for condoning all manners of pagan religions, corruption, chaos and contempt for God. As a result, she was exiled much earlier than Judah and never returned from her exile.

THE SOUTHERN KINGDOM

The Southern Kingdom, also known as Judah, had 19 kings as well. As I stated earlier, her first king was Rehoboam. He set the ground work for pagan religion and rebellion. The Bible records,

> And Solomon slept with his fathers, and was buried in the city of David his father: and Rehoboam his son reigned in his stead (1 Kings 11:43).

> And Rehoboam went to Shechem: for all Israel were come to Shechem to make him king. And it came to pass, when Jeroboam the son of Nebat, who was yet in Egypt, heard of it, (for he was fled from the presence of king Solomon, and Jeroboam dwelt in Egypt;) that they sent and called him. And Jeroboam and all the congregation of Israel came, and spake unto Rehoboam, saying, Thy father made our yoke grievous: now therefore make thou the grievous service of thy father, and his heavy yoke which he put upon us, lighter, and we will serve thee.

> And he said unto them, Depart yet for three days, then come again to me. And the people departed. And king Rehoboam consulted with the old men, that stood before Solomon his father while he yet

lived, and said, How do ye advise that I may answer this people?

And they spake unto him, saying, If thou wilt be a servant unto this people this day, and wilt serve them, and answer them, and speak good words to them, then they will be thy servants for ever.

But he forsook the counsel of the old men, which they had given him, and consulted with the young men that were grown up with him, and which stood before him (1 Kings 12:1-8).

Rehoboam disregarded the counsel of the older men and listened instead to his friends to raise taxes. As a result, the kingdom was divided. (See 1 Kings 11:26-33.) Rehoboam was a wicked king but throughout Judah's history 8 out of 19 were righteous and did what was right before the Lord. Therefore, Judah lasted 186 years longer than the Northern tribes of Israel before going into exile. This proves that when righteous kings are combined with prophetic covenant reinforcers, national revival can be the result.

But God did not forget the Northern Kingdom. He sent a prophet to show the people their sins and Israel their wickedness in that they had forsaken Him, the Bread of Life.

ELIJAH—A VOICE CRYING ALOUD

In the midst of Israel's long succession of kings, there

was one king in particular, the seventh in a long line of godless kings, named Ahab, whose diabolic acts eclipsed those of all the kings who reigned before him. To further add insult to injury to the only true God, Jehovah, Ahab married the daughter of Ethbaal, the king of the Tyrians and Sidonians, whose name was Jezebel. This unholy union only served to add more gods to the already growing smorgasbord of paganism.

However, during Omri's (Ahab's father) reign, a prophet was being prepared to deliver the Word of the Lord to Israel. His name was Elijah.

His first recorded act was to pronounce judgment on Israel's seventh king, Ahab and his wicked wife Jezebel, by declaring a famine in their kingdom..

And Elijah the Tishbite, who was of the inhabitants of Gilead, said unto Ahab, As the Lord God of Israel liveth, before whom I stand, there shall not be dew nor rain these years, but according to my word (1 Kings 17:1).

Elijah prophesied there would be no rain, and the heavens were closed until he said it would rain again. During this time, drought turned the land of Israel to dust and desert. As is characteristic during times of famine, Israel's inhabitants were stricken by disease, death and starvation all because Ahab decided to travel the wicked course of his predecessors, which further drove Israel into idolatry and perversion.

31

TRIED BY FIRE

During this drought, Elijah performed many miracles, from raising the dead, casting his mantle upon the Jordan and walking upon dry ground to being fed by ravens. God used Elijah to raise the dead, rain fire from heaven, and renounce sin and then ride in a chariot of fire as he was caught up in a whirlwind to heaven. Elisha received a double portion of Elijah's anointing, raised a dead boy to life, and even in his death had enough anointing resident in his bones to raise a Moabite soldier from the dead.

Remarkably, however, the Bible never records a prophecy from these two great prophets nor does it reveal any revival that may have swept the earth during Israel's darkest hours.

I believe the turning point of Elijah's ministry and of the nation was when he repaired the broken down altars that Ahab had destroyed. He then placed 12 stones together, representing the 12 tribes that had been divided into 2 kingdoms.

Some years earlier, when he was trying to bring unity to the nation, he called fire down from heaven. As a result, the onlookers found the God of Elijah. People fell on their faces and declared Him God and the prophets of Baal, 450 in all, were killed. Even so, because the heart of the king was not changed, the prophet ran and hid. Thus, the words of the people declaring Jehovah as Lord were futile and they did not return to Him in repentance.

Elijah had cried out to the people, "How long halt ye

between two opinions?" This is what today's prophets should cry, "How long will you waver between two opinions?" (See 1 Kings 18:21.)

We are either a nation under God or a nation against God!

THE SOUND OF AN ABUNDANCE OF RAIN

Three and-a-half years later, Elijah cried out to God for rain to once again fall upon the land.

And Elijah said unto Ahab, Get thee up, eat and drink; for there is a sound of abundance of rain. So Ahab went up to eat and to drink. And Elijah went up to the top of Carmel; and he cast himself down upon the earth, and put his face between his knees, And said to his servant, Go up now, look toward the sea. And he went up, and looked, and said, There is nothing. And he said, Go again seven times.

And it came to pass at the seventh time, that he said, Behold, there ariseth a little cloud out of the sea, like a man's hand. And he said, Go up, say unto Ahab, Prepare thy chariot, and get thee down, that the rain stop thee not.

And it came to pass in the mean while, that the heaven was black with clouds and wind, and there was a great rain. And Ahab rode, and went to Jezreel (1 Kings 18:41-45).

There is a sound of an abundance of rain! The prophet Joel said, "Be glad then, ye children of Zion, and rejoice in the LORD your God: for he hath given you the former rain moderately, and he will cause to come down for you the rain, the former rain, and the latter rain in the first month" (Joel 2:23).

I believe the Lord is ready to bring the former and latter rain together in one month. There is a deluge coming. God wants to send a revival.

Ahab reigned for 22 years while Elijah and Elisha preached. Though Elijah and Elisha are recorded in the annals of church history as two of the greatest prophets that walked the planet, they never saw Israel come to God. Israel lived in the darkest regions of its nation's history without a glimpse of a move of God.

To say the morality of the king of Israel or the Christian values of a president does not have an effect on national revival is to ignore biblical history.

Everyone wants to talk about Elijah and his miracles and Elisha's double portion. But I believe if you could converse with either of these men, they wouldn't talk to you about those victories.

Instead, I surmise they would share with you how desperately they wanted a national revival for Israel. That is why they lived. That is why they preached. That is why they prayed. That is why they fasted. They wanted to see the nation's heart turned to God.

HOW DO OUR FORMER LEADERS COMPARE?

Our former President, Bill Clinton, set the tone for not

only the White House, but also the nation and the world for eight long years. Marked by scandals, controversy, conspiracy, questionable business dealings, and ethical and moral indiscretions, America became the laughingstock of most of the free world.

While prosperity set the course for the 1990's, perversion set the topic for the evening news. Sex became a commodity and the definition confusing. Such private indiscretions were not allowed to be questioned in public for, after all, what does one's private life have to do with running the country.

The 1990's brought a resurgence of the ideologies perpetrated in the 1960's when the baby boomers came of age and were no longer rebellious teenagers who questioned authority, but viable candidates for the highest office in the free world. From beginning to end, the motto, "if it feels good, do it" dominated the minds of this group.

This philosophy mirrors that of the reign of Ahab and Jezebel. The main opponents to these groups have always been the prophets and preachers who would dare question their morality.

For the most part, our own immorality wouldn't allow us to denounce such dealings too strongly because we were fearful that our own sins would find us out. Despite it all, the Bible still says, "Righteousness exalteth a nation: but sin is a reproach to any people" (Proverb 14:34).

Former President Clinton and his wife, Hillary, were masterful at spinning a form of the truth into something that would fit their agenda. But we can't blame them entirely because the majority of Americans, including Christians, helped promote them to this lofty place of leadership.

Could it be the continuing approval rating for the impeached, but not imperiled, former Chief Executive says as much about us as it does about him? Perhaps the problems facing us are not so much what is going on in the White House as what is going on in our houses.

Was one of the reasons we wanted the impeachment ordeal to end because it reflected our own moral and spiritual condition, and the longer it lasted, the more uncomfortable we became?

Former President William Jefferson Clinton is not an aberration in his generation; he is a product of it. And if he is, what does that say about the rest of us?

It has become very easy to accuse others while excusing ourselves from the same things. Why do we always want to tell someone else to put his or her toys away when we just started playing with ours?

How can we, in good conscience, demand that our family members or friends, roommates or teammates get rid of the filth under their mattresses while we hide the same things under our pillows?

How can we condemn the skeletons in other's closets when we refuse to rid our own of dust, clutter and filth? Or is conscience even a concept that anyone understands or cares about anymore?

Somewhere in the muck and mire of our own filthy rags of righteousness there seems to be a voice coming from the pavilions of glory calling us to higher ground. The question is are we listening? Is anyone arousing from their sleep?

Paul appropriately said in the book of Romans,

Another reason for right living is this: you know how late it is; time is running out. Wake up, for the coming of the Lord is nearer now than when we first believed. The night is far gone, the day of his return will soon be here. So quit the evil deeds of darkness and put on the armor of right living, as we who live in the daylight should! (13:11,12 TLB)

I believe the tide has changed once again toward lifting up our voices in petition to God for the forgiveness of our sins. This giant, called the Bride of Christ, or the church, is once again beginning to shake herself from the trappings of a sin-sick world.

Could it be that we can once again rejoice in the Scripture which says, "When the righteous are in authority, the people rejoice: but when the wicked beareth rule, the people mourn" (Proverbs 29:2)?

Among the kings of Judah, the last righteous king was Josiah. Does our recent change in power possibly reflect that we are now living in an age similar to his reign?

Could it be that we are living in a time where the righteous are once again in seats of power to influence the moral outcome of our society and the world at large, culminating in one final and glorious outpouring of God's Holy Spirit? What is next for America?

Chapter Three

What is Next for America?

Ibelieve God has been strategically positioning us for the greatest reformation which has the potential to spawn the greatest revival in the history of the world. Revivals have come and gone over the past centuries. But nothing, I believe, will compare with what lies before us.

We have the benefit of mass media, the internet, television, radio, shortwave radio, not to mention teleconferencing and other vast resources of communication to transmit the Gospel of Jesus Christ around the world.

The question remains, "Are we ready?" Truth lies fallen in the streets, but could it be that America is on the brink of taking the next step forward to carrying the truth of the Word of God to the four corners of the earth?

For a moment, let us look at the eight righteous kings who reigned in Judah and how God used them to affect change during their reign.

A LINEAGE OF RIGHTEOUS KINGS

Asa, whose name meant "physician," removed the Sodomites. He believed God for deliverance from a one-million-man Ethiopian army. Azariah, the prophet, spoke to Asa to lead the nation out of apostasy. When he obeyed the word of the prophet and removed the idols and rebuilt the altars of the Lord, revival followed. Asa died from a disease of the feet, trusting physicians instead of God.

King Jehoshaphat, whose name meant "Jehovah judges," made peace with Israel and was in alliance with both King Ahab and Ahaziah of Israel. He was reproved by the prophet Jehu for this unholy alliance but was commended for his reforms among the nation of Judah. As a result, a great spiritual revival followed and his kingdom was delivered from Moab, Ammon and Edom.

The third righteous king was Jehoash (or Joash), whose name meant "Jehovah supports." He was installed as king by Jehoidad, the priest, and carried out extensive temple repairs. Later, however, in an attempt to appease Hazael of Syria, he stripped the temple of its hallowed things and was then slain by his servants.

Righteous Amaziah, whose name meant "Jehovah has strength," killed his father's assassins and subdued Edom. In the end, however, he was defeated when he went to war with Jehoash of Israel.

Uzziah, "the strength of Jehovah," immediately followed Amaziah as the fifth righteous king. He did well early in his reign, but later he became proud and tried to make an offering as a priest. He was judged for this act by being struck with leprosy. The prophet, Isaiah, received his call the year Uzziah died. (See Isaiah 1:1, 6:1.)

Jotham, whose name meant "Jehovah is upright," Uzziah's son, was also upright before the Lord. During his reign, he rebuilt the Upper Gate of the temple, but was opposed by Rezin, king of Syria and Pekah, king of Israel.

The seventh noble king was Hezekiah, whose name meant "Jehovah is strength." He reigned for 29 years during which time he repaired the temple, observed Passover, reinstated God's priests, and broke off relationship with Assyria.

It was also during Hezekiah's tenure that Jerusalem was besieged and miraculously delivered. He later showed Babylon's ambassadors the treasures of his kingdom which provoked God. As a result, Hezekiah fell sick, but after appealing to the prophet Isaiah, God supernaturally healed him.

Truth always has an enemy and one of its biggest foes can be time itself. Consider that in the first generation revealed truth is characterized by a conviction without compromise. In the second generation conviction clouded by complacency becomes but a belief. It may perhaps be a persuasion but not a passion. By the third generation, truth has become but an opinion open to debate. But if truth is protected it will overcome every power of the adversary.

Here we find the last righteous king ready to take his position of authority among God's people and lead them into one last great reformation.

JEHOVAH SUPPORTS

The final or eighth righteous king of Judah, out of her 19

kings, was righteous Josiah. His rise to the throne was prophesied over 300 years earlier.

> And, behold, there came a man of God out of Judah by the word of the Lord unto Bethel: and Jeroboam stood by the altar to burn incense.
>
> And he cried against the altar in the word of the Lord, and said, O altar, altar, thus saith the Lord; Behold, a child shall be born unto the house of David, Josiah by name; and upon thee shall he offer the priests of the high places that burn incense upon thee, and men's bones shall be burnt upon thee (1 Kings 13:1,2).

Josiah ascended the throne at the tender age of eight. During Josiah's reign, Judah only experienced peace. It was in the eighth year of his reign, "while he was yet young," that Josiah began to seek the Lord. This, in itself, was a miraculous feat seeing that his father, Amon, wickedly despised the Lord.

> Josiah was eight years old when he began to reign, and he reigned in Jerusalem one and thirty years. And he did that which was right in the sight of the Lord, and walked in the ways of David his father, and declined neither to the right hand, nor to the left.
>
> For in the eighth year of his reign, while he was yet young, he began to seek after the God of David his

father: and in the twelfth year he began to purge Judah and Jerusalem from the high places, and the groves, and the carved images, and the molten images (2 Chronicles 34:1-3).

In his twelfth year as king, Josiah began to purge Judah and Jerusalem of its high places and tear down the graven images. He did not let up until all of the groves were torn down and no trace of idolatry was left.

In Josiah's eighteenth year, he then took upon himself to repair the temple and, in the process, discovered the book of the law.

Josiah reigned for 31 years. His contemporary preacher was Jeremiah. This reformation was the greatest in the history of Judah, for he was the only king to do all that the Lord commanded, including tearing down the high places of worship. What happened during Josiah's reign that made national reformation take place?

THE PROPHET, PRIEST AND KING

Josiah surrounded himself with men endowed with a true desire for complete dedication and consecration to God. Thus, the combination of the prophet, priest and king's anointing brought a reformation. God brought Josiah, the king, Jeremiah, the prophet and Hilkiah, the high priest, together to spark the greatest revival in Judah's history.

As king, Josiah restored order and morality to government and the people over which he ruled. Hilkiah, the high

priest, served as the people's representative before Jehovah
God. Today, we have a high priest in our Lord and Savior,
Jesus Christ.

Now of the things which we have spoken this is the
sum: We have such an high priest, who is set on the
right hand of the throne of the Majesty in the heavens;

But now hath he obtained a more excellent ministry,
by how much also he is the mediator of a better
covenant, which was established upon better
promises (Hebrews 8:1,6).

Jeremiah was called to be a prophet during the thirteenth
year of the reign of Josiah. We know that he was chosen by
God even before he was born for the Bible records,

Then the word of the Lord came unto me, saying,
Before I formed thee in the belly I knew thee; and
before thou camest forth out of the womb I sanctified thee, and I ordained thee a prophet unto the
nations.

Then said I, Ah, Lord God! behold, I cannot speak:
for I am a child. But the Lord said unto me, Say not,
I am a child: for thou shalt go to all that I shall send
thee, and whatsoever I command thee thou shalt
speak. Be not afraid of their faces: for I am with thee
to deliver thee, saith the Lord.

Then the Lord put forth his hand, and touched my mouth. And the Lord said unto me, Behold, I have put my words in thy mouth.

See, I have this day set thee over the nations and over the kingdoms, to root out, and to pull down, and to destroy, and to throw down, to build, and to plant (Jeremiah 1:4-10).

Jeremiah was called to the task of preaching God's Word in order to turn the hearts of the people back to Him. In a vision from the Lord of the seething cauldron, he was made to see the condition of the people and the imminent judgment to come.

The first part of Jeremiah's discourse recorded in the Bible marks God's love for His people, His jealousy over them for turning from Him, and the impending judgment soon to follow.

Since the beginning of time, God has never forsaken His people. It is we who have forsaken Him. In His kindness, He leads us to turn our hearts toward Him. In the recesses of my mind I can almost hear Jeremiah lamenting,

It is of the Lord's mercies that we are not consumed, because his compassions fail not. They are new every morning: great is thy faithfulness.

The Lord is my portion, saith my soul; therefore will I hope in him. The Lord is good unto them that wait for him, to the soul that seeketh him.

For the Lord will not cast off for ever: But though he cause grief, yet will he have compassion according to the multitude of his mercies.

For he doth not afflict willingly nor grieve the children of men. To crush under his feet all the prisoners of the earth, to turn aside the right of a man before the face of the most High, to subvert a man in his cause, the Lord approveth not.

Who is he that saith, and it cometh to pass, when the Lord commandeth it not? Out of the mouth of the most High proceedeth not evil and good?

Wherefore doth a living man complain, a man for the punishment of his sins? Let us search and try our ways, and turn again to the Lord. (Lamentations 3:22-25, 31-40).

If there is a parallel between the reformation of Judah under Josiah and the possibility of a national turning toward God in America today, we can look forward to a significant move of God in our nation—but, I believe, it will be the last one before the judgment of God is poured out.

A CURRENT REVIVAL OF MORALITY IN GOVERNMENT

Could it be that President George W. Bush is doing the

same thing as Josiah did? Consider John Ashcroft. God has always been an integral part of his life and career. As the son and grandson of ministers, he went on to become a state attorney general, governor and U.S. senator of Missouri. Attorney General John Ashcroft displays his faith boldly on Capitol Hill beginning with Bible study each morning at 8:00 a.m. which he refers to as RAMP meetings Read, Argue, Memorize and Pray. The attendees read Scripture from a devotional book, discuss its meaning, memorize a psalm or Bible story and then close in prayer.

An Associated Press article also noted the following:

"Before being approved as Attorney General, John Ashcroft, tries to 'invite God's presence' while making crucial decisions and compares his political victories and defeats to resurrections and crucifixions.

"In his 1998 book, Lessons From a Father To His Son, . . . he makes clear his deep devotion to Christianity and details how it has shaped his lengthy public career from his view on race to his staunch opposition to abortion and support for the death penalty.

"The former Missouri governor also wrote that he was anointed before each of his gubernatorial terms, and on the evening before he was sworn into the U.S. Senate a friend brought out cooking oil for anointing when no holy oil could be found."[1]

A Washington Times article stated that during a

commencement address delivered by John Ashcroft to Bob
Jones University graduates that "America was founded on
religious principles, and 'we have no king but Jesus.'"[2]

Could it be possible that with this President, this Senate,
this Congress, this Supreme Court, and a strong prophetic
voice raised by us and others, prayer may return to schools?
Will vouchers bring financial breakthroughs to Christians and
private schools? Will the killing and cry of innocent babies
finally be stopped and silenced?

A GREAT SPIRITUAL AWAKENING

A *Christian History* article noted that it is important to
recognize the particular cycle a revival takes and that it most
likely includes the following facets:

1. Awakenings are usually preceded by a time of spiritual depression, apathy and gross sin, in which a majority
of nominal Christians are hardly different from the
members of secular society, and the churches seem to
sleep.

2. An individual or small group of God's people
becomes conscious of their sins and backslidden condition, and vows to forsake all that is displeasing to God.

3. As some Christians begin to yearn for a manifestation
of God's power, a leader or leaders arise with prophetic
insights into the causes and remedies of the problems,

and a new awareness of the holy and pure character of
the Lord is present.

4. The awakening of Christians occurs: many understand
and take part in a higher spiritual life.

5. An awakening may be God's means of preparing and
strengthening His people for future challenges or trials. [3]

The last decade was certainly marked by a period of spiritual decline. As prosperity and materialism abounded, our
need for God seemed to diminish. The church began looking
and acting so much like the world that it was hard to tell the
difference.

But God always has a remnant who are cognizant of their
sins. These are they who begin to desire the presence of the
Lord again and seek to cleanse themselves of their ungodly
ways. It is these who are able to say, "Who shall ascend into
the hill of the Lord? or who shall stand in his holy place? He
that hath clean hands, and a pure heart; who hath not lifted up
his soul unto vanity, nor sworn deceitfully" (Psalm 24:3,4).

These believers seek to replace the old hearts that have
become hardened and cold to the calling of the Lord with new
hearts of flesh and will rise up higher in His presence. They
long for what Ezekiel prophesied,

A new heart also will I give you, and a new spirit
will I put within you: and I will take away the stony
heart out of your flesh, and I will give you an heart
of flesh. And I will put my spirit within you, and

49

cause you to walk in my statutes, and ye shall keep my judgments, and do them (36:26,27).

Such noble men and women are not born. Rather, they are built by their battles, formed by their failures and promoted by their persecutions. Martin Luther King, Jr. said the ultimate measure of such a man is not where he stands in moments of comfort and convenience, but where he stands at times of challenge and controversy. It is time to rise up and seize the window of opportunity set before us. We cannot cower in the face of our adversary. "For if thou altogether holdest thy peace at this time, then shall there enlargement and deliverance arise to the Jews from another place; but thou and thy father's house shall be destroyed: and who knoweth whether thou art come to the kingdom for such a time as this" (Esther 4:14)?

Like Esther, I believe the Lord has called us to the kingdom for such a time as this. We must not back up or back down from the task at hand. God is waiting to demonstrate His power through us by making us mighty signs and wonders mete for His purpose.

THE SET TIME

Could it be that our set time for deliverance has come? The Psalmist said, "Thou shalt arise, and have mercy upon Zion: for the time to favour her, yea, the set time, is come. For thy servants take pleasure in her stones, and favour the dust thereof" (102:13,14).

According to many theological scholars, this passage of Scripture was written while in exile, and the set time referred to was the end of Jeremiah's seventy years, when Israel was hoping for the beginning of a brighter day.

As I stated earlier, the morality of the king seems to relate directly to the morality of the nation.

However, all the legislation in the world for godly principles will not do any good if the church stays in her lackadaisical stupor. No government agency will do for us what God alone can.

We need some Christians who will rise up with strength and anointing and stand for what is right. We need some Christians who understand they don't have to sing another song, pray another prayer, shout another shout, or dance another dance to be able to walk the high way of holiness

What we need are not only some politicians in place that will do what is right in the eyes of the Lord, but also some preachers who will point their fingers and declare the way of the Lord.

God is just looking for someone to deliver the message of salvation and hope from the chains that bind saint and sinner alike. He needs a voice, or a preacher, who will lead the way and announce that the set time for deliverance has come.

We have an opportunity that has not been afforded to us for over fifty years. The Bible says, "From the days of John the Baptist until now, the kingdom of heaven has been forcefully advancing, and forceful men lay hold of it" (Matthew 11:12 NIV).

The prize is reserved not for those who begin, but for the

finishers of the race who will not be denied their position, delayed in their pursuit, or detoured on the pathway to their promise.

This is the time for our prophets and preachers to stand up to be seen and speak loud to be heard. This is the time to put the pressure on.

Chapter Four

Where Are the Preachers?

We may have an unprecedented privilege for God to bring boldness to today's preachers and combine it with a government that recognizes God in its heart. These preachers will not preach for the applause of men or for popular opinion. Their messages will not reflect the pulse of the people but will be birthed upon their knees as their prayers ascend into the pavilions of God.

You may say, "Well, I am not a preacher so this chapter doesn't pertain to me." My response is that you are misguided. Regardless of your station in life, God has given you and me a mandate to pray for our preachers.

What most Christians don't understand is, we have to give birth to preachers and prophets in our prayer closets. We have to give birth again to the prophetic unction of the Lord Jesus Christ in the earth.

The price of neglecting to pray and not becoming the Aarons and Hurs for our pastors, apostles, prophets, evangelists and teachers has the potential result of men and women who are depleted of spiritual strength because of the many demands placed upon them. Robbed of power from on high, these leaders become an easy target for attack from the enemy.

We need prophets instead of playboys in the pulpit. We need conviction with no compromise. We need a group of men and women called into the service of the Lord birthed into the earth who will cause the gates of hell to tremble.

It is time we lift up the arms of our preachers once again; otherwise, we will become as lost sheep having no shepherd. We need to pray, "God give us some preachers again!"

THE PREACHER OF UNPOPULAR OPINIONS

Without a fresh word and a fresh baptism of Holy Ghost fire endued upon the leadership in the pulpits, how can we expect those in the pews and in our government to be any different from what they witness Sunday after Sunday in our churches across America? Jeremiah agonized,

My people have been lost sheep. Their shepherds led them astray and then turned them loose in the mountains. They lost their way and didn't remember how to get back to the fold. All who found them devoured them and said, "We are permitted to attack them freely, for they have sinned against the Lord, the God of justice, the hope of their fathers" (50:6,7 TLB).

Jeremiah was a preacher who cared more about the condition of the souls of men than the condition in which he and his family lived. Though he did seem to have moments of reprieve and even honor from some leaders, in general, he was scorned, spat upon, and before his death, his eyes were plucked from his head. His heart broke for the masses and his spirit wept for the lost.

The book of Hebrews describes the demise by which most of the bygone heroes of the faith, like Jeremiah, came to expect and experience:

Some were laughed at and their backs cut open with whips, and others were chained in dungeons. Some died by stoning and some by being sawed in two; others were promised freedom if they would renounce their faith, then were killed with the sword.

Some went about in skins of sheep and goats, wandering over deserts and mountains, hiding in dens and caves. They were hungry and sick and ill-treated—too good for this world.

And these men of faith, though they trusted God and won his approval, none of them received all that God had promised them; for God wanted them to wait and share the even better rewards that were prepared for us (Hebrews 11:36-40 TLB).

Unlike today's prophets whose faces don the covers of popular magazines or whose personas are sought from the mass media, the prophets and preachers of the past were, more often than not, killed for their stand against sin and wickedness. Jeremiah prophesied impending judgment even during Josiah's reign because of Judah's unrepentant heart.

In speaking about His wrath poured out upon Israel for her sins, He said through Jeremiah, "In spite of all this, her unfaithful sister Judah did not return to me with all her heart, but only in pretense, declares the Lord" (3:10 NIV).

Today our interest in the preachers and the prophets of the past is more out of curiosity than for the woes of the world. Too often we look for some new prophetic revelation into the future and care little for the agonizing of the souls entrusted to our eternal care.

How I long again for the time when preachers and so-called prophets will not play to the crowd but seek an audience of only One! Why? Because in the darkness are waiting wolves ready to devour the sheep in our folds. Charles Spurgeon said:

> There are no greater foes to sheep than wild dogs. In some regions, sheep were no longer to be found because these fierce creatures utterly devoured the flocks.
>
> The church has never had worse enemies than false teachers. Infidels and persecutors do but mild injury to her, but her heretical preachers have been as evening wolves.[1]

A NEW BREED OF PREACHER

The preachers calling us to higher standards of virtue are hard to hear in our ethical wasteland, even for those who make the effort to listen. Like humpbacked whales, they have been slaughtered to near extinction, for reasons nobody can remember. Prophets of moral decency and biblical absolutes now seem strange to us, maybe because so few of us have seen them. Without intervention, the world may not be able to find the prophets and so pass into oblivion on the way to an eternity spent in a devil's hell. But our mutual fund went up again last week, so what difference does it make?

God calls these preachers and prophets soldiers of sanctification, whose feet are shod with the preparation of the Gospel of peace and who hold in their hands the sword of the Spirit, "How beautiful upon the mountains are the feet of him that bringeth good tidings, that publisheth peace; that bringeth good tidings of good, that publisheth salvation; that saith unto Zion, Thy God reigneth" (Isaiah 52:7)!

It is time for a new breed of preacher. It is time for a preacher who is not trying to snuggle up to the media magnates. It is time for a prophet who, like John the Baptist, is ready to walk out of the wilderness eating locusts and wild honey, and say, "You didn't pay my way. I came on a mission for the King of kings and the Lord of lords."

For several years, we have had many preachers and teachers parading across the pulpits of America and the world, teaching us to call on the name of God, but few, however, were teaching us to believe. This is the problem we face: How can we call on Him whom we've not believed?

According to Romans 10:14,15, you must start with a preacher.

How then shall they call on him in whom they have not believed? and how shall they believe in him of whom they have not heard? and how shall they hear without a preacher?

And how shall they preach, except they be sent? as it is written, How beautiful are the feet of them that preach the gospel of peace, and bring glad tidings of good things! (Romans 10:14,15).

The divine edict of God to our hearts is very simple: "Call unto me, and I will answer thee, and shew thee great and mighty things, which thou knowest not" (Jeremiah 33:3).

The problem is many people attempt to call prematurely because they do not understand the process. God is a god of process, design, intention, and purpose. The universe is not spinning wildly out of control. There is purpose.

Therefore, before you can call, you must first believe. But before you can believe, you must hear.

The problem lies in the fact that, while according to Scripture, "So then faith cometh by hearing, and hearing by the word of God" (Romans 10:17), in order to hear what is being said, there must first be someone delivering a divine edict.

Again the Bible still very plainly articulates in the words of the apostle Paul, "I believed, and therefore have I spoken; we also believe, and therefore speak" (2 Corinthians 4:13).

Even at this, we are still missing the process. While many will tell you that you must hear to believe, and believe to speak, they leave out the foundational starting point—the need of a preacher.

GOD'S MAN IS AN INSTRUMENT OF HIS MESSAGE

The preacher must be the instrument upon which the very heart of God opens into communication. This man or woman of God must not preach what they think is best nor take a survey of what the people would like to hear.

The preacher must not preach for a preconceived conclusion. The preacher must not preach for the applause of the people. The preacher must preach what, "Thus saith the Lord."

Charles Finney said, "Great sermons lead the people to praise the preacher. Good preaching leads the people to praise the Savior."[2]

There is no greater drama in the world than the sight of a lonely preacher. He doesn't have many friends because he isn't in a popularity contest and he doesn't preach for the week's opinion polls.

I was intrigued by George W. Bush's acceptance speech at the Republican National Convention. He said, "I'm not going to be dictated in policy by the polls."

Give us some preachers of steadfast character. Give us some men who know what they believe, and the if the crowd doesn't like it, too bad. I like what A.W. Tozer said, "We are not diplomats but prophets, and our message is not a compromise but an ultimatum."[3]

America and the world need some preachers who will preach even when Ahab is singing in the choir loft and Jezebel is sitting on the front row. Give us some men who know that we are living in the final days of humanity.

Listen to what some great men of God had to day about the responsibilities of today's preachers. Oswald Chambers said, "A New Testament preacher . . . has to be surgical."[4] Martin Luther, the great reformer, said, "A preacher must be both a soldier and a shepherd. He must nourish, defend, and teach; he must have teeth in his mouth and be able to bite and to fight."[5] Ralph Waldo Emerson said, "A preacher should be a live coal to kindle all the church."[6]

Charles Haddon Spurgeon said the following:

However learned, godly, and eloquent a minister may be, he is nothing without the Holy Spirit. The bell in the steeple may be well hung, fairly fashioned, and of soundest metal, but it is dumb until the ringer makes it speak. And in like manner the preacher has no voice of quickening for the dead in sin, or of comfort for living saints until the divine spirit gives him a gracious pull, and bids him speak with power. Hence the need of prayer from both preacher and hearers.[7]

Instead, while preachers are preaching pabulum, the people in the pews are still in bondage. God wants to raise up some men and women who will wade out into the mess of humanity and begin to set people free!

Jesus described Himself by saying,

Verily, verily, I say unto you, He that believeth on me hath everlasting life. I am that bread of life. Your fathers did eat manna in the wilderness, and are dead. This is the bread which cometh down from heaven, that a man may eat thereof, and not die.

I am the living bread which came down from heaven: if any man eat of this bread, he shall live for ever: and the bread that I will give is my flesh, which I will give for the life of the world (John 6:47-51).

Charles Spurgeon shared the following experience while on a fishing expedition.

From the deck of an Austrian gunboat we threw into the Lago Garda a succession of little pieces of bread, and presently small fishes came in shoals till there seemed to be, as the old proverb puts it, more fish than water. They came to feed and needed no music.

Let the preacher give his people food, and they will flock around him, even if the sounding brass of rhetoric and the tinkling cymbals of oratory are silent.[8]

Most are not interested in a sermon that lacks conviction and soothes the soul. The modern day preacher has become an expert at playing to the crowd and telling the lost what they

want to hear. The order of today's sermon is filled with semi-
nars cater to the "victim mentality." Content with calling sin
a sickness, drunkenness a disease and pornography a problem, they tickle the ears of the hearers while wandering
around in a maze of mediocrity.

But I surmise that there has to be more to this Gospel
message than a preacher that's superpowered. There has to be
more to this Christian existence, or why would Jesus have
said, "And these signs shall follow them that believe; In my
name shall they cast out devils; they shall speak with new
tongues; They shall take up serpents; and if they drink any
deadly thing, it shall not hurt them; they shall lay hands on the
sick, and they shall recover" (Mark 16:17,18).

DELIVERERS OF A WORLD IN BONDAGE

The world is our church, and God has called His preachers to put their hand on the heartbeat of humanity with
immortality coursing through its veins. Empires will crum-
ble, and stoneworks will fade into non-existence, but the work
of His preachers will last for eternity.

Preachers are not lecturers. They are old-fashioned,
Holy Ghost filled, fire-baptized deliverers of the Gospel of
Jesus Christ.

Politicians tremble in the sight of this type of prophet.
Jeremiah didn't run for political office or start a business on
the side. Instead he was persecuted, and in the end became a
martyr in order to deliver the truth of the Word of God.

My heart's cry is, "give us some men and women who

are consumed with the condition of the lost. Give us some men who can't sleep or eat for the cries of the hurting, damned and dying. Give us some men who will speak the simple salvation message again."

I believe God is preparing the hearts of men and women for this divine calling. For Jeremiah prophesied, "Turn, O backsliding children, saith the Lord; for I am married unto you . . . and I will give you pastors according to mine heart, which shall feed you with knowledge and understanding" (Jeremiah 3:14a,15).

In this age of reformation, could it be that God has divinely destined the preachers to become a deliverers of a world born in bondage. Could it be that there are still preachers seeking the face of God for lost humanity?

I believe so, as you and I are not part of an ordinary generation. You are not an ordinary person. God has saved the best wine for last and it's you!

Chapter Five

What If We Fail?

Josiah urgently sought after the Lord in his day for His house and the inhabitants of Judah. Second Kings 23:25 states he had this testimony, "And like unto him was there no king before him, that turned to the Lord with all his heart, and with all his soul, and with all his might, according to all the law of Moses; neither after him arose there any like him."

However, what caused Josiah to fail to lead the people to true revival? He was unable to turn the hearts of the people back to God and stay His hand of judgment because of the sins of the former kings Amon and Manasseh. It was Manasseh who restored the high places of Baal, which his father had destroyed, built altars to other various gods in the courts of the temple, constructed an image of Asherah in God's house and dedicated his own son to Moloch. In all of these degenerate acts he beguiled Israel to sin.

Josiah was unable to decontaminate the land of the contagious disease of spiritual corruption. Immediately after his death, unrestrained apostasy again ran rampant among God's people because there was no true change of heart.

The consequence is found in 2 Kings 23:26, "Notwithstanding the Lord turned not from the fierceness of his great wrath, wherewith his anger was kindled against Judah, because of all the provocations that Manasseh had provoked him withal."

The preaching of a prophetic voice can change the hearts of the people. However, in all of Josiah's reformations it is important to note that they did not experience true revival. Though the people adhered to the law of God outwardly, inwardly they were still full of dead men's bones.

CAN WE LEGISLATE MORALITY?

As America and the world grow older, we know more but we are certainly not wiser. From homosexuality, physician-assisted suicide, education, abortion, family values, pornography to religious freedom, our liberties are ever so slowly being legislated to near extinction.

What if we fail, as God's people, to turn the tide from sin to the Savior?

As the gavel of our judicial system strikes another blow to truth, liberty and justice, so I hear the ringing of God's gavel in the courts of heaven as He stands ready to judge the heart of this nation and its citizens.

Many today say we can't legislate morality. Could it be that past experience reveals that possibly we are unable to change the laws of the land? Why? No one wants to lead the charge to confront the current politically correct causes of the day.

Therefore, it has become illegal to pray before a sporting event. However, our children can have sex in the backseat of a car and use the condoms the school counselor gives them.

To post the Ten Commandments in an office or school is unconstitutional because it might offend the atheist, agnostic or so-called religious leaders. When did it become unconstitutional to be offended? The Bible says, "Unto you therefore which believe he is precious: but unto them which be disobedient, the stone which the builders disallowed, the same is made the head of the corner, and a stone of stumbling, and a rock of offence, even to them which stumble at the word, being disobedient: whereunto also they were appointed" (1 Peter 2:7,8).

Such severe laws also demand a selfless accountability to God and to others. We have banned God's divine law as we exalt ourselves as gods to judge His Word. Like Lucifer, we have been deceived into exalting ourselves as equal to the Most High.

When same sex unions are sanctioned, prostitution is promoted as a "profession," the Ten Commandments are considered controversial, homosexuality is deemed discriminatory, prayer is perceived as an imposition and rebellion runs rampant—then we are at risk to become a barren nation where the mighty protection and provision of God betray us. For "righteousness exalteth a nation: but sin is a reproach to any people" (Proverb 14:34).

If we fail in our mission, could it be we might suffer the same fate as Sodom and Gomorrah—two cities that did not even have God's law?

How long then can we stay God's hand of judgment against the most "prosperous nation" on earth? How long can we wander in a maze of mediocrity singing, "Amazing Grace" as innocent lives are ripped from their mother's wombs?

As a nation, we have stooped so low that the standards we once held so high now lay beneath our feet. Someone once said if we stand for nothing, we will fall for anything. I dare say, we are rolling in the filth of our own sin-sick nature. As a society, we have become satisfied with safeguarding the status quo.

FURTHER SIGNS OF OUR TIMES

Further signs that we are living in the last days can be found within our own borders. International terrorism has taken a backseat to home grown terrorism. 2 Timothy 3:1-5 states,

> This know also, that in the last days perilous times shall come. For men shall be lovers of their own selves, covetous, boasters, proud, blasphemers, disobedient to parents, unthankful, unholy, without natural affection, trucebreakers, false accusers, incontinent, fierce, despisers of those that are good, traitors, heady, highminded, lovers of pleasures more than lovers of God; having a form of godliness, but denying the power thereof: from such turn away.

On the anniversary of the Waco debacle, April 19, 1995

a few minutes before 9 a.m. CDT, Timothy McVeigh lit the fuse on a fertilizer bomb and parked the Ryder truck carrying it outside the Alfred P. Murrah Federal Building in downtown Oklahoma City, Oklahoma. The bomb exploded at 9:02 a.m., killing 168 people and injuring hundreds more.

Over six years later on June 14, 2001 at 7:14 a.m. CDT, McVeigh walked stone-faced to the execution chamber to face death by lethal injection for his part in the bombing. In a final handwritten statement, McVeigh penned these words from the poem entitled "Invictus" written by William Ernest Henley:

> Out of the night that covers me,
> Black as the Pit from pole to pole,
> I thank whatever gods may be
> For my unconquerable soul.
>
> In the fell clutch of circumstance
> I have not winced nor cried aloud.
> Under the bludgeonings of chance
> My head is bloody, but unbowed.
>
> Beyond this place of wrath and tears
> Looms but the Horror of the shade,
> And yet the menace of the years
> Finds, and shall find, me unafraid.
>
> It matters not how strait the gate,
> How charded with punishments the scroll,
> I am the master of my fate:
> I am the captain of my soul.

"Invictus" is the Latin word for unconquered. Without remorse, except for "the collateral damage" of the children killed in the bombing, Timothy McVeigh closed his eyes and entered the other side of eternity.

Indeed McVeigh was the captain of his own fate. However, he was deceived into believing that there was no heaven or hell. The Bible says, "There is a way that seemeth right unto a man, but the end thereof are the ways of death" (Proverb 16:25).

What most people do not know about Timothy McVeigh was that he experienced a life in which his parents fought the majority of the time and eventually divorced. He was raised in a one parent home most of his life. By all accounts, McVeigh was an agnostic just like the writer of the poem he recounted.

Am I excusing his actions? Definitely not. My greatest concern is how many more McVeighs are there whom we have failed to reach? How many young boys and girls have we failed to show the love of Jesus and point to the cross of Calvary?

CONSIDER THE FACTS

Abortion, deemed as a legitimate form of birth control, though on the decline, has become more diabolical in its efforts to snuff out the lives of the innocent. Partial-birth abortion, hailed as a last resort to save a mother's life or discard the potentially physically or emotionally disabled "fetus," is viewed by many as perfectly normal and acceptable.

On April 10, 2001 the Netherlands became the first nation to legalize "mercy killings." Thus, physician-assisted suicide is deemed an appropriate action to terminate those in society who are determined to be terminally ill or judged no longer capable of functioning in society. But don't count America out of the running to kill its own. The state of Oregon has legalized euthanasia and other states are considering it as well.

We have become gods in our own eyes, capable of deciding the viability of a human life. Like Adolf Hitler, we practice a form of "cleansing" of the weakest and most vulnerable. We have taken it upon ourselves to assume the responsibility to reach some form of utopia where the fittest are the only ones who will ultimately survive. Could it be that our current President and Congress could halt these heinous acts against our children, parents, other family members and friends?

With the divorce rate in the church competing with that of the world, we need a revival in our homes. No fault divorce, instituted over 30 years ago, became one of the biggest travesties of our time. Now, three decades later, social service professionals and family counselors readily admit that strong married families are the most important factor in raising healthy children.[1]

The homosexual agenda also attempts to undermine the traditional home by promoting same sex unions—with Vermont becoming the first state to promote such unholy matrimony. This radical legislation has forced small businesses and companies to consider and even be bullied into providing coverage for a partner.

It has also prompted a proposed marriage amendment which simply states: "Marriage in the United States shall consist only of the union of a man and a woman. Neither this constitution or the constitution of any state, nor state or federal law, shall be construed to require that marital status or the legal incidents thereof by conferred upon unmarried couples or groups." [2]

How long can we bow our heads at the table of plenty, proclaim the blessing of God, and turn a deaf ear to our brothers and sisters in Christ who are dying of starvation, persecuted and martyred around the world? How long can we pray for our own family and ignore the innumerable people careening toward the bowels of hell?

Our prayers have become ineffective, our songs empty and our sermons impotent. We live a lifestyle of lavish luxury as we pursue material prosperity—while our families are bankrupt and our souls are poverty stricken. The Spirit of God, once so rich and inviting, now eludes us. We don't even recognize that God's presence has been forsaken in our lives to satisfy our own pleasures.

I fear we have but kissed the gates of heaven and are afraid to cross over to the pavilions of glory because of our weak knees, timid hearts and selfish souls. This shameful attitude has put the mediocre saint in danger of sliding down a slippery slope toward the eternal lake of fire.

Truth, liberty and justice lay fallen at our feet. God help us for He is the only one who can . . . but then again, we are about to declare Him unconstitutional as well. Who then is left to save us from ourselves?

We're not rotten at the core, we're empty at the core. We

have no center, and the things we have been leaning upon are eroding. How much longer will we be able to stand? Do we really think a fully-funded pension or an above-average performance from our stock portfolio will help us avoid the inevitable consequences of our actions and decisions? Was morality only important, or necessary, before the Dow Jones Industrial Average broke nine thousand?

Pornography invades our homes through the Internet and our schools through their libraries. Everywhere we go, from the televisions in our living rooms to the local mall, our minds are bombarded with men and women scantily dressed in clothes that used to cause us to blush.

What is the condition of our culture when a lingerie retailer sponsors the most watched Webcast in history? Who cares about the condition of our government, our community, or our own families as long as a supermodel who struts her liposuctioned stuff gives us a thrill when we gape at her on the runway in her underwear?

The Family Research Council not long ago released a study that recorded in detail more than 2,000 reports of children and adults viewing pornography online in the public library.[3] This is a disturbing indictment on our society.

Many would not literally murder someone, commit robbery or engage in illicit sex; however, every day we watch and enjoy others who engage in the same. Ephesians 5:12,13 says, "For it is a shame even to speak of those things which are done of them in secret. But all things that are reproved are made manifest by the light: for whatsoever doth make manifest is light."

A brand new millennium is underway. I suppose that is

why we seem more concerned with the hair on our heads than the character in our hearts. We have been Rogained® and whole-grained. We have vitamins and Viagra®. Our libidos are up and our guards are down. Let the good times roll!

As all of these so-called liberties seem to expand, our religious freedoms continue on a downward spiral. There is increasing hostility both in the United States and abroad toward those who name the name of Jesus Christ as the only way for salvation. Around the world, in 1999 alone, an estimated 166,000 men and women were martyred for their faith.[4] Countries with long histories of human rights violations and religious persecution now enjoy the status of being on the United Nations Human Rights Commission—while the United States was voted off by the greatest abusers in this area.

The Lord spoke to His people through Jeremiah:

Run ye to and fro through the streets of Jerusalem, and see now, and know, and seek in the broad places thereof, if ye can find a man, if there be any that executeth judgment, that seeketh the truth; and I will pardon it.

And though they say, The Lord liveth; surely they swear falsely.

O Lord, are not thine eyes upon the truth? thou hast stricken them, but they have not grieved; thou hast consumed them, but they have refused to receive correction: they have made their faces harder than a rock; they have refused to return.

Therefore I said, Surely these are poor; they are foolish: for they know not the way of the Lord, nor the judgment of their God.

I will get me unto the great men, and will speak unto them; for they have known the way of the Lord, and the judgment of their God: but these have altogether broken the yoke, and burst the bonds (Jeremiah 5:1-5).

Like an estranged spouse, the church has separated herself from her groom. I hear Jesus calling, "Return to Me, your first love." If we will but hear His bidding and repent, I believe He will heal our land.

THERE IS HOPE

We've done more than lost our moral compass—we have deliberately thrown it overboard, along with anyone who has the courage to remind us where we are supposed to go or why we set sail. In the meantime, we turn up the volume and break open another bottle of rum. We don't want some internal alarm to disturb us, let alone the preacher, while the new wave of Christian praise and worship is playing. After all, it's our favorite song. Pay no attention to the deck that has shifted under our feet again. There are no reports of icebergs in this vicinity.

I believe we really do have a seat of morality, an internal radar, so to speak, that can help us find our way. But how can the pinging of our consciences compete with the incessant howls of our unrestrained and insatiable desires, harmonizing with the siren songs of multimillion dollar ad campaigns? The way is unfamiliar and our guides unreliable, but as long as we can hear a lively tune and have money to spend or borrow, we follow the music.

We need to apply to our morals a physics lesson every preschooler learns on the playground. It is far easier to go down the slide than to go up. If you try to return the same way you came, which looks like the easiest route, the next slider will clobber you before you make much progress.

How can a world-class moral meltdown be avoided? To do so will require a repudiation of the monstrous cousins of materialism and humanism that promised to make us masters of our own fate, but instead mastered us. We have been enticed by evil and lured by lust into our enemy's territory— without the proper armor to cover us from incoming attacks. In addition, we must have a heartfelt and wholesale return to moral standards that, although imperfectly applied, have enabled us to come this far.

I'm not suggesting we turn over a new leaf, or make another resolution to do better. I'm referring to a revolutionary renewal of culture-shaking proportions that can only come from a region beyond ourselves, a renewal that is spiritual and not secular in its scope.

Perhaps I am too simpleminded in a complex age. But somehow I believe we were all better served when there were clear distinctions between right and wrong, good and evil, darkness and light, and there were people with enough conviction to make clear decisions about which was which.

In years gone by, critics ridiculed the cut-rate quality of B-grade western movies, but at least we knew the bad guys were the ones in black hats. These days, we have only conventional wisdom and political correctness to help us.

We entered the new millennium at the precipice of a decision to repent and repudiate the evils that threaten us. We must choose whether or not to continue in the humanistic hedonism that will eventually plunge us into a moral abyss from which there will be no return. We have an opportunity to experience reformation and revival such as was in the days of Josiah of Judah. Whether or not we will take advantage of that opportunity remains to be seen.

DEFEAT IS NOT AN OPTION

God will not discard His people in the day when there seems to be the greatest spiritual drought. The prophet Elijah, after experiencing one of the greatest victories of his ministry when he slew the 450 prophets of Baal, still ran and hid in fear for his own life. First Kings chapter 19 records,

And he said, I have been very jealous for the Lord God of hosts: because the children of Israel have forsaken thy covenant, thrown down thine altars, and slain thy prophets with the sword; and I, even I only, am left; and they seek my life, to take it away.

And the Lord said unto him, Go, return on thy way

to the wilderness of Damascus: and when thou comest, anoint Hazael to be king over Syria: And Jehu the son of Nimshi shalt thou anoint to be king over Israel: and Elisha the son of Shaphat of Abel-meholah shalt thou anoint to be prophet in thy room.

And it shall come to pass, that him that escapeth the sword of Hazael shall Jehu slay: and him that escapeth from the sword of Jehu shall Elisha slay.

Yet I have left me seven thousand in Israel, all the knees which have not bowed unto Baal, and every mouth which hath not kissed him (vv. 14-18).

Just like those prophets with Elijah who did not succumb to the crippling condition called compromise, God has a remnant who have refused to bow to the current moral climate of our day.

Several years ago, the Lord spoke to me and said, "I am taking the word defeat out of your vocabulary." To this day, I do not understand the meaning of failure. We must win the fight that is set before us. For as the church goes, so goes the nation and the world. Defeat is not an option.

That's why I believe that the presence of a godly king, or president, can change the laws of the land. President Theodore Roosevelt, in a speech at the Progressive Party Convention in Chicago, Illinois, said:

Just beyond man's narrow daily vision stand the immortals. "And Jehovah opened the eyes of the young man, and he saw; and behold, the mountain was full of horses and chariots about Elisha." At the front of this culture's way ride the strong guards of our own past, their authority immortalized by faithfulness. In the hour of decision we see them; their grave eyes watch us, the keepers of our standards, the builders of our civilization. They came from God to do his bidding and returned. The future we cannot see; nor what the next imperious task; nor who its strong executant. But for this generation, in a time charged with disintegrating forces, the challenge is clear: to uphold our legacy with faith, valor, and truth. . . .

Now to you men who in your turn have come together to spend and be spent in the endless crusade against wrong, to you who gird yourselves for this great fight in the never-ending warfare for the good of mankind, I say in closing, "We stand at Armageddon and we battle for the Lord."

We are in a battle for the heart and soul of America. Could it be that President George W. Bush, the current Congress and the church can lead us into the last great step which will thrust us into revival?

National revival cannot begin without personal revival. As you delve into part two of this book, I believe God has shown me, through Josiah's reign, seven vital keys that each Christian must enact personally in order to experience the same heart transformation and revival Josiah longed to see during his reign. We have just stepped into the water. Now it is time to go to the other side!

Evangelism affects the other fellow; revival affects me.

—LEONARD RAVENHILL

There can be no revival when Mr. Amen and
Mr. Wet-Eyes are not found in the audience.

—CHARLES G. FINNEY

Revival will begin when we become broken before God
and we get a lost world upon our heart.
It is our responsibility to use the giftings and
callings of God to bring revival to our city,
nation and the world.

—ROD PARSLEY

PART II

ARE WE READY FOR REVIVAL?

Chapter Six

Renew Prayer & Worship

It is not by accident that you and I were born into the age in which we currently live. It is not be mere happenstance that you are reading this book. God has a divine assignment for you.

He also has a purpose and a plan for you that will affect change not only in your neighborhood and your nation, but literally around the world. In order to begin to lead our culture in national revival, we must go back to the starting block where the 2 Chronicles records, after Josiah's ascension to the throne, his desire was to follow after the Lord.

Josiah was eight years old when he began to reign, and he reigned in Jerusalem one and thirty years. And he did that which was right in the sight of the Lord, and walked in the ways of David his father, and declined neither to the right hand, nor to the left. For in the eighth year of his reign, while he was yet young, he began to seek after the God of David his father (34:1-3).

The first key to true revival must begin with prayer. But our fast-food world and microwave culture have stripped us of our ability to prevail in prayer. Thus, we have lost the ability to stand.

We have lost the inner commitment to keep us on our knees. We have lost the ability our forefathers had of kneeling in the presence of a holy God and praying through until our burden lifted.

Without prayer, the church becomes paralyzed from doing exploits and is rendered helpless from preaching to the lost. In the end, she then implements her own plans, schedules her own revival conferences, and supplements church attendance with victims' meetings.

What is prayer? Prayer is a thought turned God-ward. Prayer is a form of worship unto God. It is a humble attitude where the believer bows his heart before the throne of Jehovah and dedicates unrivaled adoration, seeks solace and receives rest in communion with his Creator.

Prayer can be equated with a desire toward the ultimate life in God. Summed up, it is "not my will but thine be done." It is the full purpose of God in every thought, action and motive.

Authentic prayer is the source of courage and productivity, as it was for the prophets and apostles.[1] In order to pray, we must have vision that is clear, virtue that is mighty, and then we will have victory that is assured.

E.M. Bounds said, "The prayers of God's saints are the capital stock in heaven by which Christ carries on His great work upon the earth. Great throes and mighty convulsions in the world have come about as a result of these prayers. The earth is changed, revolutionized; angels move on more powerful, more rapid wings; and God's policy is shaped when the prayers of His people are more numerous and more efficient."[2]

PRAYER MUST BE OUR PRIORITY

Psalm 108:1-4 says, "O God, my heart is fixed; I will sing and give praise, even with my glory. Awake, psaltery and harp: I myself will awake early. I will praise thee, O Lord, among the people: and I will sing praises unto thee among the nations. For thy mercy is great above the heavens: and thy truth reacheth unto the clouds."

The time to get your priorities straight is during this reformation. There is no higher calling than the place of prayer. Therefore, prayer must be a priority.

This is no time to be weak in faith. This is no time to be in confusion concerning God's will for your life, your family or your country.

You and I must seek God's face in prayer so that our minds are clear and our tongues are articulate, because God is about to give us a word in season to speak to them that are weary. (See Isaiah 50:4.)

FOR MY NAME'S SAKE

After Israel had been in bondage for several years, the heathen began to question God's power among His people. In essence, they taunted, "Where is your God we have heard so much about that He is not even able to deliver you?" The Lord's response was,

> Therefore say unto the house of Israel, Thus saith the Lord God; I do not this for your sakes, O house of Israel, but for mine holy name's sake, which ye have profaned among the heathen, whither ye went.

> And I will sanctify my great name, which was profaned among the heathen, which ye have profaned in the midst of them; and the heathen shall know that I am the Lord, saith the Lord God, when I shall be sanctified in you before their eyes (Ezekiel 36:22,23).

God told his people in this passage of Scripture that His deliverance did not have anything to do with them. Let me say it this way. The divine initiative and prerogative belong to God.

You and I should not ask, "Lord, help me to pray." Instead we should ask, "Lord, help me want to pray."

The divine initiative, the prompting, must come from God. Otherwise, all you have is the dead letter of religion. It must spring forth to life out of rivers of living water, that proceed out of your belly. (See John 7:38.) When it comes that way, then there is an anointing and power upon your prayers.

We must pray that God would make us His willing servants. We must want to do what God wants us to do. For it is in Him we live, and move, and have our being. (See Acts 17:28.)

Therefore, if you are led into prayer it must be Him that does the leading. Scripture bears this out, "When thou saidst, Seek ye my face; my heart said unto thee, Thy face, Lord, will I seek" (Psalm 27:8).

It is not you who makes a determination to seek the things of God. Rather, it is God who is in you both to will and to do according to His own good pleasure. (See Philippians 2:13.)

Our spirit, indeed, is willing, to seek the Lord but our flesh is weak. (See Matthew 26:41.) This means that the flesh is weak in its desire to follow after the Spirit. The struggle is not in your spirit, because your spirit came directly from God. Your spirit is always ready to do that which the Holy Spirit desires that you do.

The problem is most Christians do not spend time nourishing their spirits; therefore, they are in a weakened condition. Although the spirit is willing, it is not strong. Rather, the flesh is strong.

That is why the Bible says, "For bodily exercise profiteth little: but godliness is profitable unto all things, having promise of the life that now is, and of that which is to come" (1 Timothy 4:8). Many exercise their bodies but few take the time to exercise their spirits.

Your flesh is weak in its ability to respond to the divine

initiative. Therefore, you must harness your flesh. You must render your flesh ineffective. You must say to your flesh, "You are the servant. You are good for nothing but to get my spirit to where it needs to be!"

According to the Word, "Every man that striveth for the mastery is temperate in all things. Now they do it to obtain a corruptible crown; but we an incorruptible. I therefore so run, not as uncertainly; so fight I, not as one that beateth the air: but I keep under my body, and bring it into subjection: lest that by any means, when I have preached to others, I myself should be a castaway" (1 Corinthians 9:25-27).

As I shared earlier, God was about to take Israel (this motley-looking crew who had messed up and fallen short) and sanctify Himself in them. Allow me to interject this here: God can use you and me regardless of how we have messed up our lives.

The Lord will take you out of your problems and promote you to a position of authority. He will lift you up from your burden. He will set you above depression and discouragement, because He has need of you!

I WILL YET BE ENQUIRED OF

Ezekiel 36:37,38 states, "Thus saith the Lord God; I will yet for this be enquired of by the house of Israel, to do it for them; I will increase them with men like a flock. As the holy flock, as the flock of Jerusalem in her solemn feasts; so shall the waste cities be filled with flocks of men: and they shall know that I am the Lord."

The only prerequisite for God's deliverance is that we must ask Him to do it. Though God's heart is to do all of these things for you so that His name could be glorified in the earth, even yet He is bound by His word. Can you see God being restrained by His word? He wants to give us a miracle, but His Word that states "He must be asked" holds Him back.

Jesus said it this way, "Hitherto have ye asked nothing in my name: ask, and ye shall receive, that your joy may be full" (John 16:24).

He said it another way in Mark 11:22-24, "And Jesus answering saith unto them, Have faith in God. For verily I say unto you, That whosoever shall say unto this mountain, Be thou removed, and be thou cast into the sea; and shall not doubt in his heart, but shall believe that those things which he saith shall come to pass; he shall have whatsoever he saith. Therefore I say unto you, What things soever ye desire, when ye pray, believe that ye receive them, and ye shall have them."

First John says it this way. "And this is the confidence that we have in him, that, if we ask any thing according to his will, he heareth us: And if we know that he hear us, whatsoever we ask, we know that we have the petitions that we desired of him" (5:14,15).

My question to you is, "When are you going to ask the Lord for what you need?" This is the hour that God will do what He promised. The only prerequisite is that you must ask Him.

GOD'S PROMISES BECOME OUR PRAYERS

Matthew Henry's Commentary on Ezekiel 36 states:

By asking for the mercy promised we must give glory to the donor, express a value for the gift, own our dependence, and put honour upon prayer which God has put honour upon.

Christ himself must ask, and then God will give him the heathen for his inheritance, must pray the Father, and then he will send the Comforter; much more must we ask that we may receive. They must consult the oracles of God, and then also God is sought unto and enquired after. The mercy must be, not an act of providence only, but a child of promise; and therefore the promise must be looked at, and prayer made for it with an eye of faith fastened upon the promise, which must be both the guide and the ground of our expectations.[3]

Notice what he said, "The matter of God's promise must become the matter of our prayers." In other words, we need to get a word concerning our situation, and then stand upon it. If the Lord said He will give us the heathen for an inheritance, we must confess it. If He said He will bless us financially, then we must refuse to believe otherwise.

One of the major reasons the body of Christ fails to receive that for which they requisition the throne of God is because, "Ye lust, and have not: ye kill, and desire to have, and cannot obtain: ye fight and war, yet ye have not, because ye ask not" (James 4:2).

The aforementioned commentary stated that even Jesus must ask. Jesus said in the Gospel of John, "And I will pray the Father, and he shall give you another Comforter, that he may abide with you for ever" (14:16). He did not presume upon the Father to do it, even though He knew it was the Father's will to do it.

Why did Jesus, the Son of Man, have to ask God for anything? He had to ask while He was on this earth because He came to the earth as a man, not deity humanized or humanity deified. Therefore, as a man on the earth, He had to operate as you and I do.

If Jesus had to ask, how much more do you and I have to ask? Jesus could not presume upon the will of the Father. A great man of God said, "It is yet to be seen what could happen through one consecrated life that would allow God to do that through them which He desires." Jesus had to pray the Father, and then, and only then would the Comforter come.

Look at what happens, according to Matthew Henry's Commentary, when we petition God in the courts of heaven. First, we give glory to the donor. We have the misconception that when we ask the Father and He answers, that then we glorify Him. What we miss is that in the asking, we have glorified Him.

Second, we express a value to the gift. This means if you and I are going to expend the spiritual, mental, and physical time in prayer necessary to express our need before God, then we show Him that we highly regard that for which we are asking.

Third, our asking shows that we place our dependence upon God. We are saying to God, "If you don't answer my prayer, then there can be no victory."

Finally, we put honor upon prayer which God has put

honor upon already. In other words, we esteem the value and importance of prayer as highly as our heavenly Father does.

THE HOUSE OF PRAYER

Once our personal lives become temples of prayer, it is only fitting that prayer will become foremost in the house of God. Isaiah 56:7 says, "Even them will I bring to my holy mountain, and make them joyful in my house of prayer: their burnt offerings and their sacrifices shall be accepted upon mine altar; for mine house shall be called an house of prayer for all people."

Rather today, our churches have become a place of great preaching. They have become a sanctuary filled with good, but not necessarily anointed, singing. The parish has become a board room to vote on the newest hymnals. The temple has become a retreat for thieves and robbers.

The Bible records, "And they come to Jerusalem: and Jesus went into the temple, and began to cast out them that sold and bought in the temple, and overthrew the tables of the moneychangers, and the seats of them that sold doves; And would not suffer that any man should carry any vessel through the temple. And he taught, saying unto them, Is it not written, My house shall be called of all nations the house of prayer? but ye have made it a den of thieves" (Mark 11:15-17).

E.M. Bounds said, "Prayer is perfectly at home in the house of God. It is no stranger, no mere guest; it belongs there. It has a peculiar affinity for the place, and has, more-over, a Divine right there, being set, therein, by Divine appointment and approval. The inner chamber is a sacred place for personal worship. The house of God is a holy place for united worship."[4]

In the posture of prayer pride surrenders.
In the place of prayer passions die.
In the presence of prayer the power of the Holy Ghost in all of His manifestations is birthed.
In the purpose of prayer we petition heaven for the heathen. We appeal to the throne for our daily bread. We plead for revival lest we perish.

WE ARE THE GENERATION WHO WILL SEEK HIM

Who shall ascend into the hill of the Lord? or who shall stand in his holy place? He that hath clean hands, and a pure heart; who hath not lifted up his soul unto vanity, nor sworn deceitfully.

He shall receive the blessing from the Lord, and righteousness from the God of his salvation. This is the generation of them that seek him, that seek thy face, O Jacob. Selah (Psalm 24:3-6).

I believe we are the generation who must traverse the mountain of the Lord into the holy place.

Prophetically, I have shared with you that we are living in a moment when the current equivolents of Josiah and Hilkiah and Jeremiah can all unite their forces and affect a national revival that will shake the forces of darkness around the world.

The Bible declares that I should not sin against you by failing to pray for you. No one has to be prompted to criticize, but everyone has to be prompted to pray.

We must have a promise which becomes the road map for what we are expecting from the Lord. We are looking toward that promise with eyes of faith in the arena of expectation.

The doctor's report is not our guide. The stock market is not our guide. The evening news is not our guide.

This is no time to compromise our position of opportunity in America or the world by succumbing to a prayerless life. This is no time to negotiate at the table of our adversary. Just like Josiah, this is a time to stand up to be seen, to speak loud to be heard, and to do that which is right in the eyes of the Lord.

Second Chronicles 7:14 says, "If my people, which are called by my name, shall humble themselves, and pray, and seek my face, and turn from their wicked ways; then will I hear from heaven, and will forgive their sin, and will heal their land."

Jeremiah 29:13,14 declares, "And ye shall seek me, and find me, when ye shall search for me with all your heart. And I will be found of you, saith the Lord: and I will turn away your captivity, and I will gather you from all the nations, and from all the places whither I have driven you, saith the Lord; and I will bring you again into the place whence I caused you to be carried away captive."

We must not let up now. We need to pray as never before. If you have ever entered into the closet of intercession, it is more imperative now than ever before that you do so. Our family prayer altars must become a priority once again.

During our services, worship must lead us into prayer for a national revival. Our music must not be an opportunity for entertainment. Instead it must lead us into intercession. Our songs must place us upon our faces before God in a pool of tears, calling upon His name, thanking Him for His wondrous works, and glorifying Him for what He's already done. My heart's cry is, "Oh, God, let us return to the closet of prayer!"

Chapter Seven

Restore God in Government

The worship of idols among God's people was prevalent in both the Northern and Southern kingdoms of Israel. It did not matter that God's law explicitly forbade such practices. The book of Exodus chronicles the following words,

Thou shalt have no other gods before me. Thou shalt not make unto thee any graven image, or any likeness of any thing that is in heaven above, or that is in the earth beneath, or that is in the water under the earth:

Thou shalt not bow down thyself to them, nor serve them: for I the Lord thy God am a jealous God, visiting the iniquity of the fathers upon the children unto the third and fourth generation of them that hate me; And shewing mercy unto thousands of them that love me, and keep my commandments (20:3-6).

The practice of idol worship permeated the culture, and the so-called requests of these pagan gods were both ruthless and merciless.

PAGAN GODS AND PERVERSE PRACTICES

Some of the most worshiped gods during the early part of Josiah's reign were Moloch, Asherah, Topheth and Chemosh.

Moloch was the national deity of the Ammonites. (See Leviticus 18:21; Jeremiah 32:35.) The worship of Moloch was characterized by parents sacrificing their own babies— piercing them through with poles and setting them on fire to serve as light for the people's godless celebration. (Gehenna, another name for hell, was formed with special reference to the children offered as burnt sacrifices to this image. It signifies hell and hell-fire.)

Asherah was a goddess of the Canaanites, who represented sex and war. Her symbol was a pole or tree and her fetish was legalized vice. Lust and murder were glamorized as part of the ritual of sacrifice from those who worshiped her. On a fragment of the Baal Epic, she is shown, "wading ecstatically in human gore up to her throat—all the while exulting sadistically."[1]

This same justification for lasciviousness and disregard for the sanctity of marriage could be seen in the adulterous acts of our former president, Bill Clinton, and the moral voice, Jesse Jackson.

Topheth was worshiped by the Canaanites and later by

Israel. (See Psalm 106:38; Jeremiah 7:31.) This deity was especially exalted by Manasseh. The name, "Topheth," was "commonly supposed to be derived from the word, 'drum' used to drown the cries of children who were made to pass through the fires to Molech. Some regard Topheth as from 'contempt,' or 'the place of burning dead bodies.'"[2]

Chemosh was the national god of the Moabites and Ammonites. (See Judges 11:24; 2 Kings 23:13.) This pagan image was associated with heavenly bodies. This gives credence to the thought that there is nothing "new" about the new age movement. It is still an occult practice birthed from ancient idol worship. Like Moloch, Chemosh was worshiped by the sacrifice of children as burnt offerings. Solomon included the worship of this deity to show his acceptance for all religions. (See 1 Kings 11:7.)

These were the same pagan idols Josiah destroyed:

And in the twelfth year he began to purge Judah and Jerusalem from the high places, and the groves, and the carved images, and the molten images.

And they brake down the altars of Baalim in his presence; and the images, that were on high above them, he cut down; and the groves, and the carved images, and the molten images, he brake in pieces, and made dust of them, and strowed it upon the graves of them that had sacrificed unto them.

And he burnt the bones of the priests upon their altars, and cleansed Judah and Jerusalem. And so did he in the cities of Manasseh, and Ephraim, and Simeon, even unto Naphtali, with their mattocks round about.

And when he had broken down the altars and the groves, and had beaten the graven images into powder, and cut down all the idols throughout all the land of Israel, he returned to Jerusalem (2 Chronicles 34:3b-7).

The removal of idols began the cleansing of the land from pagan worship. The second key that we must institute in order to witness revival is the restoration of God in our government.

THE TURNING TIDE OF ABORTION

On November 3, 1870, an editorial entitled, "The Least of These Little Ones," written by editor, Louis Jennings, a conservative Christian, appeared in the New York Times. Following is an excerpt:

It is useless to talk of such matters [abortion] with bated breath, or to seek to cover such terrible realities with the veil of a false delicacy. In impudent defiance of all morality, law, and decency a trade of murder is known and acknowledged to be practiced in our midst. Can it be that the social degeneracy, which follows political corruption like its shadow, has already overtaken us, and that we have become callous to the plague-spots that infect society? Has the flaunting vice, on which our [city] rulers smile, deadened the public sense of all goodness and decorum, and lowered our standards of social morality? The fact would not be without example if it were so; but unless on the strongest evidence, we cannot accept such a conclusion.

Respectable citizens have merely ceased to express indignation, because of a mistaken belief in their utter powerlessness. From a lethargy like this it is time to rouse ourselves. The evil that is tolerated is aggressive; if we want the good to exist at all, it must be aggressive too. The ax is laid to the tree of corruption which threatens to overshadow us, and there are strong and willing hands enough to strike it home, if they were roused to a consciousness of their power[3]

Just over 100 years later, in 1973, in the landmark U.S. Supreme Court case of *Roe versus Wade* that legalized abortion that same newspaper said, "A major contribution to the preservation of individual liberties . . . it wisely avoids the judicial quicksand of attempting a judicial pronouncement on when life begins."[4]

If we were nothing more than a worthless blob before we were born, why did the Psalmist write,

For thou hast possessed my reins: thou hast covered

me in my mother's womb. I will praise thee; for I am fearfully and wonderfully made: marvellous are thy works; and that my soul knoweth right well.

My substance was not hid from thee, when I was made in secret, and curiously wrought in the lowest parts of the earth. Thine eyes did see my substance, yet being unperfect; and in thy book all my members were written, which in continuance were fashioned, when as yet there was none of them (139:13-16).

There is an ominous warning for the voter and congress-men alike who allow the legislation of murder. Joel 3:19 says, "Egypt shall be a desolation, and Edom shall be a desolate wilderness, for the violence against the children of Judah, because they have shed innocent blood in their land."

The church is hanging on to her moral foundation by only the slenderest of threads. When the multitudes of those who name the name of Christ are in conflict over supporting an agenda that includes a wrong as monstrous as partial-birth abortion, it is time to dial a spiritual 911 for a dying church. Surely judgment is at the door. Ruin or resurrection are the only options.

Dr. James Dobson, psychologist and host of the popular radio program *Focus on the Family* said,

The truth is that we are responsible for the tragedy of the Clinton presidency. Many in the church remained silent when he vetoed the ban on partial-birth abortion. We looked the other way when he courted and granted enormous political power to homosexuals who sought to destroy the traditional family. We hardly uttered a peep of protest when he vetoed the marriage penalty tax, which discriminates against husbands and wives living in committed, legal relationships.

More indicting is the fact that millions of Christians didn't even bother to vote in 1992 or 1996 when Clinton was given power. People living in a democracy get the government they deserve, and we share the blame for the disaster of the past eight years. . . We cannot merely point a detached finger of accusation at the immoral behavior of our president when we stood by and let it happen!

During the National Right to Life Convention's annual prayer breakfast this year, Father Frank Pavone of Priests for Life noted that the number of American babies lost to abortion every day would be equal to the following events: 5 TWA 800 crashes, 7 Oklahoma City bombings, and 110 Columbine shootings.[5]

A new poll by Zogby American Values shows that a majority of Americans (51%) believe "abortion destroys a life and is manslaughter." Only 35 percent think "abortion does not destroy a life."[6]

Could it be that the polls show a shift is occurring in public opinion toward life? Could it be that there is a change coming?

Mark 9:42 says, "And whosoever shall offend one of these little ones that believe in me, it is better for him that a millstone were hanged about his neck, and he were cast into the sea."

On January 22, 2001, the 28th anniversary of Roe versus Wade, the tide of the slaughter of our unborn began to turn. On this day, pro-life advocates held their annual "March for Life" protesting the 1973 Supreme Court decision which legalized abortion. Also, that very same day, President George W. Bush signed an executive order which put a stop to funneling federal tax dollars into international family planning institutions which were used to create abortion clinics globally.

His predecessor, William Jefferson Clinton, signed a bill into law that allowed federal agencies to give away millions of tax dollars a year so that other nations could have abortion clinics.

In a written statement, read by New Jersey Republican Representative Chris Smith, Bush said the promise of a right to life, liberty and the pursuit of happiness in the Declaration of Independence "is for everyone, including unborn children."

"We share a great goal, to work towards the day when every child is welcomed in life and protected by law," Bush said. "We know this will not come easily, or all at once. But the goal leads us onward: to build a culture of life, affirming that every person, at every stage and season of life, is created equal in God's image."[7]

Wouldn't you rather see your tax dollars go to support the church and their efforts to feed the hungry, clothe the naked, and house the homeless instead of to support abortion clinics around the world?

In response to this unprecedented move, Austin Ruse, President of the Catholic Family & Human Rights Institute (C-FAM), issued the following statement: "President Bush's decision to reinstate Mexico City language sends a strong and immediate message to the world that the United States will no longer be at the forefront of spreading abortion to countries that do not want it."

"Mexico City language, decided upon by the Reagan administration in 1984, prohibits American taxpayer money from supporting groups that perform or lobby for abortion in foreign countries. Most United States funds have been funneled through the United States Agency for International Development, which directly supports groups that both perform abortions and lobby foreign governments to change abortion laws.[8]

ONLY PARTIAL VICTORY

Father Richard John Neuhaus, editor-in-chief of the periodical *First Things*, said that Clinton will be described in the history books as "The Abortion President."[9]

Why? Twice he vetoed a bill that would outlaw the heinous and pain-inflicting procedure of partial-birth abortion. The truth is that more than 70 percent of the American people oppose partial-birth abortion.[10]

Though former President Clinton seemed to be moved by opinion polls of his sexcapades, he was not, however, moved by the public's opinion of partial-birth abortion!

Partial-birth abortion is a barbaric procedure by which

fully viable and unanaesthetized infants are murdered during the final moments of delivery. Unfortunately, the U.S. Supreme Court in the case of *Stenberg versus Carhart*, in a 5-4 ruling said that this hideous atrocity could not be banned.

One of the dissenting justices, Supreme Court Justice Clarence Thomas offered this opinion about the ruling, "From reading the majority's sanitized description, one would think that this case involves state regulation of a widely accepted routine medical procedure. Nothing could be further from the truth. The most widely used method of abortion during this stage of pregnancy is so gruesome that its use can be traumatic even for the physicians and medical staff who perform it . . . and the particular procedure at issue in this case, 'partial-birth abortion,' so closely borders on infanticide that 30 states have attempted to ban it."

During a partial-birth abortion, a child in the third trimester of gestation is brought three-fourths of the way out of its mother's womb. With the base of its head exposed, and scissors implanted in the back of its skull, this little one's brain is extracted by suction.

In the meantime, doctors of debauchery solicit the organs of those aborted children, who, in their eyes, do not warrant the common decency of a simple burial. The price for these body parts varies on the basis of the age of the infant when aborted. No wonder billion dollar businesses have sprung up! As Americans are fulfilling the demand for these tiny organs, treating it as though selling the parts of murdered children is comparable to selling the parts from used cars.

But our future children have this hope: President George W. Bush, in his acceptance speech at the Republican National

Convention boldly stated, "And when Congress sends me a bill against partial-birth abortion, I will sign it into law."

FROZEN IN TIME

Not only do we rip our children from their mothers' wombs; but also, frozen in time, we seek to further destroy our seed by dissecting them in the embryonic stage. After all, frozen embryos are of no use to anyone.

Former Surgeon General, Joycelyn Elders, once told pro-lifers to "get over their love affair with fetuses."[11]

Why not dispose of these embryos just like we do aborted babies—in our own dumpsters? After all, since the legalization of abortion, the crime rate has steadily dropped for the past 18 years!

The reasoning, some so-called experts say, is because the legalized abortion of 27 million unborn babies has contributed to the reduction of teenagers, who, if they had been allowed to be born, presented a tendency and even a high risk toward a life of crime.

Syndicated columnist, George Will said, "Talk about covert operations. The liberal left and other abortion on demand advocates appear to be systematically attempting to reduce crime rates by convincing you to murder your baby because statistically he/she has a higher probably of committing a violent crime."[12]

Let us remember the words of our Lord and Savior, Jesus Christ. "One day some mothers brought their babies to him to touch and bless. But the disciples told them to go away. Then Jesus called the children over to him and said to the disciples, 'Let the little children come to me! Never send them away! For the Kingdom of God belongs to men who have hearts as trusting as these little children's. And anyone who doesn't have their kind of faith will never get within the Kingdom's gates'" (Luke 18:15,16 TLB).

FAITH-BASED INITIATIVES

Not only does it appear that the tide is turning in support of the lives of our unborn children, but could it also be that our President and government is beginning to see the tremendous work most churches across America do to help those in need?

A recent poll found that 75 percent of Americans favor allowing religious groups to apply for federal grants to deliver social services.[13]

The four major proposals that will allow faith-based organizations to obtain funds are:

1. Allow faith-based groups to receive money under the federally funded after-school program 21st Century Learning Centers.
2. Provide start-up funds for projects serving people.
3. Establish mentoring programs for children of prisoners.
4. Set up programs to help broken families.[14]

At the time of this writing, on Thursday, July 19, 2001, Congress took the all important step to expand charitable giving and end discrimination against these armies of compassion by passing the Faith-Based and Community Initiative.

Several months earlier, President Bush created an office in the White House to coordinate federal cooperation with private and religious charities.

"When we see social needs in America, my administration will look first to faith-based programs and community groups, which have proven their power to save and change lives," Mr. Bush said before signing the executive order to create the office. "We will not fund the religious activities of any group, but when people of faith provide social services, we will not discriminate against them."

Mr. Bush also signed an executive order that will begin to remove bureaucratic barriers to cooperation with religious charities. It creates offices in five federal departments—Justice, Housing and Urban Development, Health and Human Services, Labor, and Education—to examine policies and regulations that inhibit such cooperation.

Throughout the campaign, Mr. Bush promised to **"mobilize the armies of compassion"** by making it easier for religious based charities to compete for federal money.

Mr. Bush said religious organizations can provide a

wide variety of services that would otherwise be provided by local and federal government, including child and adult day care, drug treatment, food banks, and homeless shelters.[15]

Could it be that like Josiah, the President, senate and congress are beginning to take notice once again that this nation was built upon the foundation of Christian ethics? Could it be that we are once again going to be a nation that declares proudly, "In God We Trust"?

Chapter Eight

Repair God's House

It had been nearly 250 years since the last temple had been restored under Joash. (See 2 Kings 12:4-16.) The house of God was in great disarray because of all of the former idolatrous kings. Throughout the years they had allowed the temple to become run down and even further desecrated with pagan idol worship.

I can only imagine the condition that God's holy temple was in. I can picture the weeds growing up through the cracks in the earth around its entrance. I can almost see the result of years of war and desolation that had taken their effect upon this beautiful edifice. I can also envision the images of many pagan gods cluttering and corrupting this holy place. Now, mostly abandoned, the temple was more like a tomb. But there came a king, Josiah, who was ready to restore and repair the habitation of God, His temple, once again.

Now in the eighteenth year of his reign, when he had

purged the land, and the house, he sent Shaphan the son of Azaliah, and Maaseiah the governor of the city, and Joah the son of Joahaz the recorder, to repair the house of the Lord his God.

And when they came to Hilkiah the high priest, they delivered the money that was brought into the house of God, which the Levites that kept the doors had gathered of the hand of Manasseh and Ephraim, and of all the remnant of Israel, and of all Judah and Benjamin; and they returned to Jerusalem.

And they put it in the hand of the workmen that had the oversight of the house of the Lord, and they gave it to the workmen that wrought in the house of the Lord, to repair and amend the house (2 Chronicles 34:8-10).

The third key to national revival is to "Repair God's House." I believe today, however, that this refers not to a physical rebuilding of an outward edifice or structure, but to repairing the temple of our own hearts.

AN EMPTY HOUSE IS TARGET OF INVASION

Time and time again the temple of the Lord was invaded by enemy forces throughout the reign of the kings of both Israel and Judah. Many times it was completely destroyed only to be rebuilt again. The precious and holy things were constantly stolen or misused. The temple's structure and contents suffered greatly.

Like any house, if it is not lived in, it eventually begins to suffer disrepair and neglect. A house that is left in that state is also subject to invasion. Consider the words of Jesus in the Gospel of Matthew as He parallels our bodies to houses.

> When the unclean spirit is gone out of a man, he walketh through dry places, seeking rest, and findeth none.

> Then he saith, I will return into my house from whence I came out; and when he is come, he findeth it empty, swept, and garnished.

> Then goeth he, and taketh with himself seven other spirits more wicked than himself, and they enter in and dwell there: and the last state of that man is worse than the first. Even so shall it be also unto this wicked generation (Matthew 12:43-45).

Throughout America and the world, the past and present have been marred by a disregard for the church and Christians. As God's redemptive souls, we have an obligation to live above the blight of sin that plagues us.

We have profaned the living temple with dead idols for which there can be no agreement. The holy cannot make the unholy like itself. But the unholy can profane the holy. Like the Pharisees, we have been more concerned with cleaning the outside of the bowl while leaving the inside unwashed.

We cannot shed any tears for the innocent child slain while still in the womb for, surely, we are not responsible. We cannot warn the sinner in their sin because we might be labeled a "religious fanatic." We cannot love the lost because our lust refuses to allow us to do so. We cannot heal the brokenhearted for our own hearts have become cold and void of the presence of God.

We cannot deliver those who are bound when we ourselves are not free. We cannot help the hopeless, love the unlovable, or heal the hurting for we have more pressing matters to take care of.

We cannot grasp the horns of the altar, and with unspeakable groanings cry, "Forgive me, a sinner." For after all we are the "righteousness of God."

CONTEMPORARY CHRISTIANS

The church has evolved into a congregation of contemporary Christians with our temple unfit for a King. Contemporary Christians are entertained by contemporary music void of the blood, the cross and, above all, the name of Jesus.

Contemporary Christians seek after express worship services in a microwave society to fit into their busy schedules. Contemporary Christians are motivated by a user friendly Gospel which keeps them shouting, clapping, dancing and singing but certainly lacks conviction.

Contemporary Christians ask, "What can you do for me?" instead of, "How can I help you?" Contemporary

Christians are prompted by position. They seek the most stately seats in the sanctuary, the praise of the preacher and the power of popularity.

Contemporary Christians are nothing more than puppets placating to the devil's most diabolical scheme to defile the temple, desecrate our altar and destroy the atmosphere for God's presence to dwell in us richly.

During the prophet Haggai's time, the temple of God was also left in disarray for the Bible records:

> Then came the word of the Lord by Haggai the prophet, saying, Is it time for you, O ye, to dwell in your cieled houses, and this house lie waste? Now therefore thus saith the Lord of hosts; Consider your ways.

> Ye have sown much, and bring in little; ye eat, but ye have not enough; ye drink, but ye are not filled with drink; ye clothe you, but there is none warm; and he that earneth wages earneth wages to put it into a bag with holes.

> Thus saith the Lord of hosts; Consider your ways. Go up to the mountain, and bring wood, and build the house; and I will take pleasure in it, and I will be glorified, saith the Lord (Haggai 1:3-8).

It is time to rise up and repair God's temple, the temple of our hearts. It is time to put away the idols that have polluted the places of God's dwelling. Until we can begin to cleanse our own houses, we cannot expect the type of culture-shaking revival that America and the world needs.

Today most Christians, especially those in America, are not required to watch over their temples with due diligence. Instead they overindulge their flesh, overcompensate for their weaknesses, and their minds are overcome with unclean thoughts.

Therefore, it is enough for us to simply be ridiculed to quench the fire in our souls. The jeers of co-workers are sufficient to silence our witness. The threat of tauntings and teasings lead us to tame our tongues.

We need to have the testament of Ignatius, one of the early church fathers, who was martyred to attest to this truth that we are the temples of the living God. On his way to be devoured by lions, he wrote to the church at Rome:

> Now I begin to be a disciple. I care for nothing, of visible or invisible things, so that I may but win Christ. Let fire and cross, let the companies of wild beasts, let breaking of bones and tearing of limbs, let the grinding of the whole body, and all the malice of the devil, come upon me; be it so, only may I win Christ Jesus!

> And even when he was sentenced to be thrown to the beasts, such was the burning desire that he had to suffer, that he spake, what time he heard the lions roaring, saying, "I am the wheat of Christ: I am going to be ground with the teeth of wild beasts, that I may be found pure bread."

If, for our witness, we are led on to the lion's den God will be with us. And, then we will begin to be His disciples.

Under Josiah's rule, repair was desperately needed, and he set about to see it accomplished during his reign. Today, however, we need to repair the temple of our hearts in order to house the glory of the Lord.

YE ARE TEMPLES OF THE LIVING GOD

In the New Testament, God no longer dwells in houses made with hands. For Acts 7:48 says, "Howbeit the most High dwelleth not in temples made with hands." We made the transition from the physical temple to a spiritual temple housed within our mortal body.

And what agreement hath the temple of God with idols? for ye are the temple of the living God; as God hath said, I will dwell in them, and walk in them; and I will be their God, and they shall be my people.

Wherefore come out from among them, and be ye separate, saith the Lord, and touch not the unclean thing; and I will receive you (2 Corinthians 6:16, 17).

Just as the Jewish temple preparations were meticulous and great, in that it was designed and erected by decree of the divine Architect, and when finished separated from ordinary functions, so our body, or temple, should be consecrated to Jehovah with the greatest regard. Therefore, we are temples of the living God.

As the Christian offers up his or her life as a living temple where God can dwell, his or her whole life becomes a continual sacrifice before the Lord. This is our just service.

It is a complete defection from the world and the things in the world. That is why this passage of Scripture says that there can be no agreement with idols. This is not to say that we should live as a hermit. Jesus said we were to be in the world but not of it.

Jesus, Himself, was led into the wilderness only to be tempted by the devil. Later He prayed for His disciples, "I pray not that thou shouldest take them out of the world, but that thou shouldest keep them from the evil" (John 17:15).

God does not want us to be so earthly minded that we are of no heavenly good. Neither does He want us to be so heavenly minded that we are rendered ineffective to Him while on earth. As the temple of God, the Lord seeks for us to be consistent in our walk with Him regardless of where we represent Him—whether it be in the church, our place of business, school or when we are with our family.

WE ARE A HOUSE OF PRAYER

As the temple of God in the Old Testament was a house of prayer, so should we, "as living temples," be houses of prayer. Thus, as the Jewish temple was furnished to reflect a place of worship, so should our lives be consecrated for this holy service. For it is from the altars of hearts that we are commanded to offer up a sacrifices of praise, giving thanks unto the name of the Lord. (See Hebrews 13:15.) Those who worship God, "lifting up holy hands without wrath or doubting," are then transformed into priests of God.

As I shared in key number one to revival, "Renew Prayer and Worship," in the temple of God, the house of prayer, everything else becomes insignificant and Christ alone is the center of our worship. With Christ as the focal point, we are unable to stray from the highway of holiness unto the road of temptation.

God wants us, His temples, to be houses of prayer. When we commune with Him in our everyday life, He becomes Lord of all. As Lord, He is highly exalted above every principality and power that would try to establish their lordship illegally in our lives.

THE LORD HAS PLACED HIS NAME

The temple of God is also the place where the Lord has placed His name and approved of its holiness. Deuteronomy 26:2 says it this way,

> That thou shalt take of the first of all the fruit of the earth, which thou shalt bring of thy land that the Lord thy God giveth thee, and shalt put it in a basket, and shalt go unto the place which the Lord thy God shall choose to place his name there.

How glorious to have the name of Jehovah God recorded over the doorposts of our hearts and to inhabit our tabernacles! We are then chosen to be His holy habitation and royal priesthood!

How do we know that the Lord has placed His name upon the tabernacle of our hearts? Do we have this testimony?

And these signs shall follow them that believe; In my name shall they cast out devils; they shall speak with new tongues; They shall take up serpents; and if they drink any deadly thing, it shall not hurt them; they shall lay hands on the sick, and they shall recover.

So then after the Lord had spoken unto them, he was received up into heaven, and sat on the right hand of God. And they went forth, and preached everywhere, the Lord working with them, and confirming the word with signs following. Amen (Mark 16:17-20).

When we are the Lord's temples and His name is engraved upon our hearts, our high priest is Jesus Christ, and we have the fulfillment, "To whom God would make known what is the riches of the glory of this mystery among the Gentiles; which is Christ in you, the hope of glory" (Colossians 1:27).

The God in Christ has become the Christ in us which is the hope of our glory! When we have this hope, we can do all things through Him who strengthens us. When we are weak, Jesus is strong. Our lives are possessed with the Spirit of the living God who is able to cause us to love and serve Him because He is at work within us!

RESTORE THE BROKEN DOWN WALLS OF OUR LIVES

Like Nehemiah, we need to restore the broken down walls of our habitations.

So built we the wall; and all the wall was joined together unto the half thereof: for the people had a mind to work.

And it came to pass from that time forth, that the half of my servants wrought in the work, and the other half of them held both the spears, the shields, and the bows, and the habergeons; and the rulers were behind all the house of Judah. They which builded on the wall, and they that bare burdens, with those that laded, every one with one of his hands wrought in the work, and with the other hand held a weapon (Nehemiah 4:6,16,17).

We need to rise up and work with the weapon of the Word in one hand and a tool in the other hand. This is no time to sit idly by and allow the philosophies and wisdom of the world to defile our temples.

Notice that when the children of Israel began to repair the

house of God, the money for the restoration came from the people. Not only did their funds provide for the restoration of the temple, but they also provided for the upkeep as well. We need to do the same thing as the children of Israel and repair our own houses.

In order to see the lost saved, initiate faith-based programs, feed the hungry, clothe the poor and restore some sense of dignity to people around the world who have suffered tremendous material and physical loss, the body of Christ needs to learn how to give again.

GOD'S HOUSE RESTORED

While the children of Israel were in Babylonian captivity, Cyrus, the King of Persia, was especially anointed by God to return His people to their own homeland. In an unheard of move by a pagan king who didn't even worship God, he commanded the people:

> Thus saith Cyrus king of Persia, The Lord God of heaven hath given me all the kingdoms of the earth; and he hath charged me to build him an house at Jerusalem, which is in Judah.

> Who is there among you of all his people? his God be with him, and let him go up to Jerusalem, which is in Judah, and build the house of the Lord God of Israel, (he is the God,) which is in Jerusalem.

And whosoever remaineth in any place where he sojourneth, let the men of his place help him with silver, and with gold, and with goods, and with beasts, beside the freewill offering for the house of God that is in Jerusalem.

Then rose up the chief of the fathers of Judah and Benjamin, and the priests, and the Levites, with all them whose spirit God had raised, to go up to build the house of the Lord which is in Jerusalem. And all they that were about them strengthened their hands with vessels of silver, with gold, with goods, and with beasts, and with precious things, beside all that was willingly offered (Ezra 1:2-6).

You will notice that these men did not go to Jerusalem empty handed but instead were laden with gold, silver, precious jewels, and everything necessary to repair the house of the Lord. The treasure heaped up by Babylonian kings over the years was placed into Cyrus' hands to then transfer to the children of God.

This is very important for us today because where our treasures are, there will our temples be also. Then, when we begin to repair our temples and cleanse them, they are ready to be dedicated and, I believe, we will experience what happened in the days of Solomon:

And it came to pass, when the priests were come out of the holy place, that the cloud filled the house of the Lord, so that the priests could not stand to minis-

ter because of the cloud: for the glory of the Lord
had filled the house of the Lord.
Then spake Solomon, The Lord said that he would
dwell in the thick darkness. I have surely built thee
an house to dwell in, a settled place for thee to abide
in for ever (1 Kings 8:10-13).

God will begin to fill us with His glory and presence in a
greater way and we will begin to experience a revival of
unprecedented proportions!

Chapter Nine

Revive the Biblical Principles of Giving

Michael Novak illustrated, over 25 years ago, in his thought-provoking book, *The Spirit of Democratic Capitalism*, "that a society's wealth or financial well-being can be demonstrated to be geared amazingly close to its theological worldview."[1]

The fourth key Josiah initiated to spark reformation was the revival of the biblical principles of giving. Let's look again at 2 Chronicles 34:8-10 and verses 11-13:

> Now in the eighteenth year of his reign, when he had purged the land, and the house, he sent Shaphan the son of Azaliah, and Maaseiah the governor of the city, and Joah the son of Joahaz the recorder, to repair the house of the Lord his God.

> And when they came to Hilkiah the high priest, they delivered the money that was brought into the house

of God, which the Levites that kept the doors had gathered of the hand of Manasseh and Ephraim, and of all the remnant of Israel, and of all Judah and Benjamin; and they returned to Jerusalem.

And they put it in the hand of the workmen that had the oversight of the house of the Lord, and they gave it to the workmen that wrought in the house of the Lord, to repair and amend the house.

Even to the artificers and builders gave they it, to buy hewn stone, and timber for couplings, and to floor the houses which the kings of Judah had destroyed.

And the men did the work faithfully: and the overseers of them were Jahath and Obadiah, the Levites, of the sons of Merari; and Zechariah and Meshullam, of the sons of the Kohathites, to set it forward; and other of the Levites, all that could skill of instruments of musick.

Also they were over the bearers of burdens, and were overseers of all that wrought the work in any manner of service: and of the Levites there were scribes, and officers, and porters.

A HELPING HAND

King Josiah realized during the 18th year of his reign that

if any real change was going to transpire in his kingdom and in the social climate of the people, it was going to be wrought in the house of the Lord. Therefore, he initiated a plan to help the church do the things that the church is supposed to do instead of being a roadblock to everything the church tried to do.

The people of Israel then commenced to repair the house of the Lord. However, in order to make the necessary repairs, an offering needed to be taken from the people. The people took the offerings and put them in the hands of the priest. Deuteronomy 26:3,4 states,

> And thou shalt go unto the priest that shall be in those days, and say unto him, I profess this day unto the Lord thy God, that I am come unto the country which the Lord sware unto our fathers for to give us. And the priest shall take the basket out of thine hand, and set it down before the altar of the Lord thy God.

The priest took the money that was at the doors and in turn gave it to the workmen who were to repair the house of the Lord. God is not unfaithful to provide for the people of God. He will even provide from unlikely sources!

LAST WORDS ARE IMPORTANT

In the Book of Malachi, the last book of the Old Testament, God was getting ready to silence the heavens for 400 years. Last words are important.

Will a man rob God? Yet ye have robbed me. But ye say, Wherein have we robbed thee? In tithes and offerings.

Ye are cursed with a curse: for ye have robbed me, even this whole nation.

Bring ye all the tithes into the storehouse, that there may be meat in mine house, and prove me now herewith, saith the Lord of hosts, if I will not open you the windows of heaven, and pour you out a blessing, that there shall not be room enough to receive it.

And I will rebuke the devourer for your sakes, and he shall not destroy the fruits of your ground; neither shall your vine cast her fruit before the time in the field, saith the Lord of hosts.

And all nations shall call you blessed: for ye shall be a delightsome land, saith the Lord of hosts (3:8-12).

The first question God asks is, "Will a man rob God?" This question sends your mind immediately to the thought that you are taking something away from God. The fact of the matter is, what you are robbing the Lord of is His ability to be who He covenanted to be in your life—Jehovah Jireh, your Provider and Rewarder.

Hebrews 11:6 says, "But without faith it is impossible to please him: for he that cometh to God must believe that he is, and that he is a rewarder of them that diligently seek him."

God is not a rewarder of casual acquaintances. He is not a rewarder of those who meander in the world and come into service on Sunday and act spiritual. He is, however, a rewarder of those who diligently seek Him. All the deliverance God ever brings is brought by a seed.

Malachi goes on to say how the people robbed God, and it was in tithes and offerings. What is the tithe? It is not whatever amount you think appropriate or what you can afford. The tithe is ten percent of the sanctified gross income. That is the commandment.

An offering is your option. It's not an option whether or not you give an offering. It is an option of how much of an offering you choose to give.

A NATIONAL CURSE

Malachi 3:9 goes on to say, "Ye are cursed with a curse." Notice God did not say, "I have cursed you," but He said, "You are cursed . . . for you have robbed me, even this whole nation."

The situation is this: it was an individual sin that brought about a national curse. Everyone within the nation of Israel did not rob God. However, because there were those in the nation who did in fact rob Him by withholding their giving, the whole nation fell under a curse.

Many in today's churches respond to this passage of Scripture by saying, "Well, it really doesn't have anything to do with me." I must retort that someone else is always influenced by another person's transgression.

Take, for instance, at the battle of Ai. Joshua 7:1 says, "But the children of Israel committed a trespass in the *accursed* thing: for Achan, the son of Carmi, the son of Zabdi, the son of Zerah, of the tribe of Judah, took of the accursed thing: and the anger of the Lord was kindled against the children of Israel."

The firstfruits are sanctified unto the Lord. Abraham offered the first fruits, or ten percent, from his slaughter of the five kings to Melchizedek four hundred years before the law was instituted.

Deuteronomy 8:18 bears out that we must give our firstfruits in order that God's covenant may be established in the earth.

First, Israel lost the battle because they were affected by the disobedience of one person, namely Achan. Second, they committed a national sin. As I stated earlier, Malachi 3:9 says, "Ye are cursed with a curse: for ye have robbed me, even this whole nation." Third, everyone did not go to battle. Last, Joshua did not properly communicate the vision.

BRING ALL THE TITHE INTO THE STOREHOUSE

God's commandment to begin the blessing process was, "Bring ye all the tithe into the storehouse." (See Malachi 3:10.)

Today, some Christians don't feel as though they are getting fed spiritually where they go to church. The music just doesn't seem to have quite the anointing that it used to have. It's as though they don't feel the presence of the Lord like they used to.

My response to them is that the first thing a person should do is to check their giving. You can only get out what you put in. You can only withdraw that which you have deposited.

Did you notice that God does not have an "s" on the end of "storehouse?" Therefore, He did not mean storehouses.

The storehouse in your life is wherever you receive your regular spiritual nourishment. I shared with you in the last chapter that it is a place where the Lord has placed His name and signs follow them. (See Mark 16:17-20.)

When you give scripturally, you're not giving away from yourself because you will most likely need to make a withdrawal from the preacher's anointing one day. The Bible says, "He that receiveth a prophet in the name of a prophet shall receive a prophet's reward; and he that receiveth a righteous man in the name of a righteous man shall receive a righteous man's reward" (Matthew 10:41).

Why do we bring all of the tithe into the storehouse? Malachi bears out that it is so there may be meat in God's house.

The prophet, Amos, declared that, "Behold, the days come, saith the Lord God, that I will send a famine in the land, not a famine of bread, nor a thirst for water, but of hearing the words of the Lord: And they shall wander from sea to sea, and from the north even to the east, they shall run to and fro to seek the word of the Lord, and shall not find it" (8:11,12).

My prayer is that our churches will be known as the "houses of bread." Where there is bread, there is healing.

Where there is bread, there is anointing. Where there is bread, there is deliverance! Where there is bread, there is meat, spiritual sustenance. Where there is water, there is the Holy Spirit present to fill, refill and quench the thirsting of the parched soul.

The church doesn't need another good idea. We don't need another church growth seminar or a nursery brainstorming session.

Just one word is all we need. For if God does not speak then we cannot advance. We need to hear a prophetic word from heaven again.

STOP IT! THAT'S ENOUGH!

The passage in Malachi goes on to say, "Prove me now herewith, saith the Lord of Hosts, if I will not open the windows of heaven and pour you out a staggering and over-whelming blessing that you can't stand up under." (See 3:10.) God will have to strengthen your legs to cause you to be able to stand up under the weight of the blessing.

The Lord continues on to say that He will rebuke the adversary for our sake. To rebuke means to say, "Stop it! That's enough!" The word "rebuke" is the same word Jesus used when standing over Peter's mother-in-law to rebuke the fever which had arrested her. (See Matthew 8:14,15.)

God's purpose through your giving is to rebuke your adversary. It's time to allow the Lord to put a stop to the devourer who is trying to ravage your finances, family, faith and future.

You and I need to be the catalyst for a nation, allowing God to proclaim through us, "Stop it! That's enough! We won't stand for immorality any longer. We won't stand for abortion any longer. We won't stand for spiritual bankruptcy any longer! We declare and proclaim, Devil, stop it! That's enough!"

If you fail to comprehend the premise for your giving, then you are just paying a bill. In reality, however, there is no bill to pay. God just wants to get you involved in His divine economy. Therefore, you must never sow a seed that you don't specifically direct it toward a need in your life.

That is why God put a seed in your hand, because the seed has life in itself. There is power in that seed to produce deliverance down the road for you. That's how God delivered the entire human race. He delivered them by making His Son, Jesus Christ, a seed.

THE REMNANT OF ISRAEL

The collections for the temple are supposed to have begun sometime earlier in Josiah's reign. (See 2 Kings 22:4.) But a very interesting anomaly occurs. The "remnant of Israel" referred to in 2 Chronicles 34:9 are those of the Northern Kingdom who had not been carried away into captivity.

Consider that when the Israelites were conquered, their entire nation was pillaged by their enemies. If they were not put to death, it was normally only the king, royalty, noblemen, scholars, and the wealthiest who were carried away into captivity after their conquest.

In the New Testament, we have the picture of a Roman soldier leading the conquered king through the streets of the city, with a cart tied behind him with all of his nation's treasures. Jesus did the same thing when He descended into hell and took back for us everything the devil has stolen. "Wherefore he saith, When he ascended up on high, he led captivity captive, and gave gifts unto men" (Ephesians 4:8).

Here in "the remnant of Israel" exists normally the poor, downtrodden, elderly and sometimes women and children. These lowly ones already regarded the temple as the one bond left of their national, as well as, religious life. Therefore, they sent their offerings for the repair of the temple in Judah. This "legal due" for the temple was known as a temple tribute which was equivalent to one day's wages a year.

A swelling tide of patriotism and religion increased their gifts, which far exceeded the legal dues. So many were the gifts and so large their gifts that they were always first brought to certain places and then to the temple. The needs of the temple were met by the generosity of the people!

THE WEALTH OF THE WICKED

President George W. Bush, as governor of the state of Texas, did a similar thing. He put more state funds into Christian organizations to help with inner city works, prisons, rehabilitation, and welfare. During the 2000 presidential campaign, he stated that he believes one of the keys to turning America around is once again to give power to church-based organizations to help the social ills of our country.

In this final hour of human history, the wealth of the government and the wealth of the wicked will be laid up for the just! (See Proverbs 13:22.) I believe God has positioned us for the greatest wealth transfer in the history of the church to take place during this final generation.

James 5 states, "Be patient therefore, brethren, unto the coming of the Lord. Behold, the husbandman waiteth for the precious fruit of the earth, and hath long patience for it, until he receive the early and latter rain. Be ye also patient; stablish your hearts: for the coming of the Lord draweth nigh (vv. 7,8).

There is a payday someday. God is drawing the curtain on the last act of human history. He is ready to bring into our hands money to finance this great Gospel message so that we can preach Jesus Christ to the far-flung corners of the world!

WE ARE DIVIDED, BUT UNITY WILL EMPOWER US

Could it be that God is waiting for a people who will put aside their petty differences and unite to overthrow the kingdom of darkness? I do believe that God is moving in this realm throughout the body of Christ, and the forces of darkness know it. That's why they so desperately fight against the church.

During the 2000 presidential election, the nation seemed to be divided right down the middle. One of the operative forces that facilitated the division was confusion. By earthly wisdom, the media, politicians, voters and the church were trying to decipher what was going on in a time when chaos ruled. The Bible says,

> But if ye have bitter envying and strife in your
> hearts, glory not, and lie not against the truth. This
> wisdom descendeth not from above, but is earthly,
> sensual, devilish. For where envying and strife is,
> there is confusion and every evil work (James 3:14-
> 16).

America was divided along racial, ethnic, socioeco-
nomic, religious and gender lines. There was no standard.
The kingdom of Israel was divided . . . just like America.

Do you know why Israel was divided? They wanted a
king. They wanted to be like every other country. Though
God wanted to be their king, He fulfilled their desire to have
an earthly king anyway.

America, today, faces some of the similar issues that
Israel faced. We want to be like everyone else. No one wants
to stand up for righteousness because they don't want to hurt
anyone's feelings. They want an "inclusive" Gospel which
dictates that some forms of sin are acceptable based upon the
politically correct standards of the day.

Earlier I shared that during the prophet Elijah's day he
cried out to the people of Israel, "How long halt you between
two opinions?" The book of James says it this way:

> If any of you lack wisdom, let him ask of God, that
> giveth to all men liberally, and upbraideth not; and it
> shall be given him. But let him ask in faith, nothing
> wavering. For he that wavereth is like a wave of the
> sea driven with the wind and tossed.

For let not that man think that he shall receive any thing of the Lord. A double minded man is unstable in all his ways" (James 1:5-8).

We need to begin to perform all of the words of the covenant again. Second Kings 23:3 says, "And the king stood by a pillar, and made a covenant before the Lord, to walk after the Lord, and to keep his commandments and his testimonies and his statutes with all their heart and all their soul, to perform the words of this covenant that were written in this book. And all the people stood to the covenant."

It is time for the body of Christ to unite under the banner of Jesus Christ again. When we do, Psalm 133 promises,

Behold, how good and how pleasant it is for brethren to dwell together in unity! It is like the precious ointment upon the head, that ran down upon the beard, even Aaron's beard: that went down to the skirts of his garments; As the dew of Hermon, and as the dew that descended upon the mountains of Zion: for there the Lord commanded the blessing, even life for evermore (vv. 1-3).

After the people fulfilled the commandment of the king to give an offering, it was then they rediscovered the word of the Lord. Across America and around the world, there will be a rediscovery of God's Word. We need to fall in love with the Bible again. Some people think it's just a good book. Some people talk about it, but they don't really love it. We need to love the words left for us by our Heavenly Father.

Chapter Ten

Rediscover the Word of God

J ohn Conley, a ranking army commander during the Vietnam War, once said to former President Lyndon Johnson, "We cannot win this war because you have never asked the American people to sacrifice."

When the priests, in Josiah's time, brought the money into the holy temple to repair it, God revealed again His Word to His people. They knew the meaning of sacrifice. This, I believe, is the fifth key to revival – rediscovering the Word of God. Second Chronicles 34:14 reveals, "And when they brought out the money that was brought into the house of the Lord, Hilkiah the priest found a book of the law of the Lord given by Moses."

The government in Josiah's time began to support and understand that if any real change was going to transpire in the social climate of the nation, it was going to be wrought in the house of the Lord. Because of this, Josiah began to endorse, or help, the church do the things it was supposed to do instead of being a roadblock to everything it tried to do.

Therefore, the southern kingdoms Judah, began to rebuild the house of the Lord. As I shared in the last chapter, as they were rebuilding the temple, they took an offering. Then when they diligently made the repairs on the house of the Lord, all of a sudden, the priest rediscovered God's Word.

But is it that America and Christians alike think of "sacrifice," as some taboo word that is hardly worth thinking upon and should never be considered to literally be acted upon?

The Bible is our standard and code of conduct. As Charles Spurgeon once said, "It is the oak of God planted in the forest of eternity, entwining its roots around the Rock of Ages." However, in our present society, we have refused to sacrifice our carnal desires to receive the heavenly blessing of delving into its pages. We've allowed those radicals in the minority who can shout the loudest to set the course for our future. Our "Christian" conduct is carnal. We've substituted the Word of Truth for false doctrine. It is time to rediscover God's Word again!

IDOLATRY BREEDS FALSE DOCTRINE

George Barna, a well-known Christian pollster, described the decline of the American character as "moral anarchy" in his book, <u>Boiling Point</u>.

According to *The Pastor's Weekly Briefing*, produced by *Focus on the Family*, this trend can be traced to a rise in "income tax cheating, the rapid growth of the pornography industry, frivolous lawsuits, rising levels of white collar crime, increased rates of co-habitation and adultery, and so forth.

"They [Barna] also suggest that the United States is now in a state of spiritual anarchy as well. The average Christian has rejected such elements as church loyalty, respect for clergy, acceptance of absolutes, reverence for God, a desire to strive for personal holiness, sensitivity to theological heresy, and appreciation of tradition, say Barna and Hatch."

"'The Christian Church is struggling to influence the nation's culture because believers think of themselves as individuals first, Americans second, and Christians third. Until that prioritization is rearranged, the Church will continue to lose influence,' said Barna."[1]

Josiah removed all idols, as I discussed in chapter four, and in doing so he removed false doctrine. There is idolatry in the church, as people literally worship preachers.

Our current culture and carnal "Christian" character ridicule the rise of moral integrity, physical purity and spiritual intensity. Instead of speaking the truth with eternal severity we entice the ears and seduce the soul with a gospel cloaked in sweet slander.

Our laws are lawlessness. Our prayers are prayerlessness. Our preaching is powerless. Our lives are lifeless. Our convictions are laced with contradictions. Our pews are full of spectators who listen to our unanointed oratory and stammering rhetoric as we proclaim a user-friendly gospel to a self-indulgent, self-seeking assembly.

Our doctrine dismisses depth. Our singing exalts empty entertainment. Our preaching promotes popularity. Our intercession lacks anguish. Our hearts are cold, our knees are feeble and our hands are weak.

I have never been more aware of my calling in this nation than I am now, and that is to bring the church of Jesus Christ back to its doctrinal senses. We need to get away from all the trite little teachings that tickle the ears and teach people nothing. So many don't even know what the blood covenant is. They don't know what the gifts of the Holy Spirit are, much less how to operate in them. They don't know what repentance from dead works is. All they know are trite, little sermons.

No wonder rebellion against so-called church leaders seems almost justified. Who wants to follow a church leader who can't keep some woman other than his wife out of bed with him? Who wants to follow a preacher that can't keep pornography magazines out from underneath the floorboard of his car?

I have good news: There's a change coming! Revival is coming to the pulpit and the pew!

THE INTERNET INFLUX

Before my pastor, mentor and friend, Dr. Lester Sumrall, left this world, he had a vision regarding the present age. He saw the devil coming through a TV screen, and he said, "I am Apollyon." This was another word or name for Satan. He then saw the devil come through a television screen and say, "I will destroy this nation through this screen."

Computers had just started to come into being when he gave that Word, and the Holy Spirit spoke up in my spirit and said that it dealt with computers also. The Internet, just like television, was meant for God, and God's own people use it for the devil.

Many have turned to it to fill themselves with its tempting doctrine left by the void of sin. They turn to "chat rooms" and take on a different identity. They seduce someone who is not their spouse into an adulterous relationship, not just in thought but literally, physically as well. Jesus said, "Ye have heard that it was said by them of old time, Thou shalt not commit adultery: But I say unto you, That whosoever looketh on a woman to lust after her hath committed adultery with her already in his heart" (Matthew 5:27, 28).

Some people have a television idol. Some people have a telephone idol. One medium dispenses gossip on a mass basis. The other is used by individuals to dispense gossip and lies.

We have come a long way from holiness. We have come a long way from a real relationship with God. This type of insatiable desire is idolatry and will send a soul to hell if not dealt with at the altar of God.

THERE IS NO HEAVEN, THERE IS NO HELL

Not long ago, I went to another city and started preaching about heaven, and they just stared at me like I was speaking in a foreign language. The reason was because their preachers in that area of the country had been telling them that they had a new revelation, and that any mention of heaven in the Bible is just figurative. There is not really a place called heaven. It just means the dwelling of God. Since we don't know where God is, we really don't know where that dwelling is.

But my Bible says, "Let not your heart be troubled: ye believe in God, believe also in me. In my Father's house are many mansions: if it were not so, I would have told you. I go to prepare a place for you" (John 14:1,2).

It was stated of Abraham, "He looked for a city which hath foundations, whose builder and maker is God" (Hebrews 11:10).

Jesus said also, "But lay up for yourselves treasures in heaven, where neither moth nor rust doth corrupt, and where thieves do not break through nor steal" (Matthew 6:20).

Heaven is mentioned 559 times in the Bible. What a terrible thing to be deceived into believing the false doctrine that heaven is not a literal place! Paul said in his letter to the church at Corinth, "If in this life only we have hope in Christ, we are of all men most miserable" (1 Corinthians 15:19).

At heaven's gate, we trade tribulation and trials of life for heaven's true riches. D.L. Moody said,

> The Christian's hope of heaven is not an undiscovered country, and the attractions of this earth cannot be compared to anything in it. Perhaps nothing but the shortness of our range of sight keeps us from seeing the celestial gates all open to us, and nothing but the deafness of our ears prevents our hearing the joyful ringing of the bells of heaven.

There are constant sounds around us that we cannot

hear, and the sky is studded with bright worlds that
our eyes have never seen. Little as we know about
this bright and radiant land, there are glimpses of its
beauty that come to us now and then.[2]

Oh, the population of heaven will greatly outnumber that
of hell! There will be those there many thought would never
make it. Some of the most abandoned will be found there.
George Whitefield once said, "There would be some in
heaven who were the devil's castaways." Some who even the
devil thought were not even good enough for him will be
there because the love of God is fathomless. The fact of the
matter is all they need is the blood of Jesus Christ.

THE CROSS—MORE THAN A SYMBOL ON A CHAIN

We have a lot of religion, singing, spaghetti dinners and
emotions, but we have very little of the cross. Without the
crimson red stain of Calvary's bleeding Lamb, church attendance is void and of no effect. Baptism and communion
mean nothing without the blood-stained cross of our crucified
Canaan King. It is the cross and nothing but the cross. It is
the Lamb of God and nothing but the Lamb of God, because
it is the blood and nothing but the blood.

A professor of theology at one of the highest acclaimed
schools of theological learning in the world once stood at a
podium with his Bible and made this stunning and staggering
announcement: "I am a liberal in theology. Of course, I do
not believe in the virgin birth, nor in the old-fashioned

doctrine of substitution and atonement. Nor do I know any intelligent Christian minister who does."

Another theologian, said as well, "Why do we speak of the death of Jesus of Nazareth? Why do we not rather speak of the death of Emerson or Emmanuel Cant, or Socrates? Jesus is not the center of our religion. One might just as well speak of the wool of the lamb as to speak of the blood."

Recently, a popular preacher said, "I don't think that anything has been done in the name of Christ or under the banner of Christianity that has proven more destructive to the human personality, and hence, counterproductive to the evangelism enterprise, than the often crude, uncouth, and un-Christian strategy of attempting to make people aware of their lost and dying condition."

When I was a small boy growing up in church I remember singing songs like, "What can wash away my sin? Nothing but the blood of Jesus. What can make me whole again? Nothing but the blood of Jesus. Oh, precious is the flow that washes white as snow. No other fount I know. Nothing but the blood of Jesus."[3]

Another song we sang was, "Years I spent in vanity and pride, caring not my Lord was crucified. Knowing that it was for me He died on Calvary."[4]

"Oh, the bliss of this glorious thought, my sin, not just part, but the whole is nailed to His cross. And I bear it no more. Bless the Lord, bless the Lord, oh my soul."[5]

Yet another song brings into full view the cross of Calvary, "When I survey the wondrous cross on which the Prince of Glory died, my richest gain I count but loss, and pour contempt on all my pride."[6]

When John Wesley was asked what must be done to keep Methodism alive when he was dead, he immediately answered, "The Methodists must take heed to their doctrine, their experience, their practice, and their discipline. If they attend to their doctrines only, they will make the people antinomians [one who rejects a socially established morality]; if to the experimental part of religion only, they will make them enthusiasts; if to the practical part only, they will make them Pharisees and if they do not attend to their discipline, they will be like persons who bestow much pains in cultivating their garden, and put no fence round it, to save it from the wild boar of the forest."[7]

If you take the blood out of the Cross of Calvary, you make salvation of no significance and certainly of no effect. The Apostle Paul said it this way in the book of Galatians, "But God forbid that I should glory, save in the cross of our Lord Jesus Christ, by whom the world is crucified unto me, and I unto the world" (6:14).

A CAUSE FOR CONCERN

The body of Christ needs help in returning to the discarded values of the past—we need to rediscover the Word of God again. We have had so much pabulum-pumping preaching and entertainment that the body of Christ is in a cesspool of powerless Christianity.

In a men's meeting where I was preaching, by estimation, at least seventy-five percent of the men in attendance were in some form of perverse, sexual bondage. It is hard to describe what it is like to be in an atmosphere of Christian men where the majority of them attest that they are bound by pornography, sexual perversions, addictions, homosexuality, and incest.

The next altar call I gave was for those with addictions to alcohol and drugs, and there were equally as many men who responded.

These were men who had enough God consciousness and loved God enough to come from all over the country to a Gospel Christian meeting. The sad fact remained though, they were sitting in church services every Sunday morning, but were bound by sexual perversions and addictions.

And these are the men. The Bible says that we are made strong by reason of the men.

No wonder we are so anemic and weak! No wonder our spiritual and moral lives are so frail! Men and women are in such states as this because the body of Christ, at large, has turned away from biblical doctrine.

We have taken the bypass. We say, "we are weak." God says, "you are wicked." We say, "we are sick." God says, "you have sinned." Adultery is no longer sin in Hollywood or in most church circles. We have produced a soft breed of Christian that must be spoon fed a steady diet of spiritual junk food, served up by some pabulum-pumping pulpiteer who himself has been selected by the backslidden church board. His promotion to the pulpit is not on the basis of his prophetic anointing, but rather on his Las Vegas ability to lead this personality cult we used to call the church.

A liar is no longer a sinner, he's an extrovert with a lively imagination. We have allowed politicians to institute a welfare system that legitimizes illegitimacy. The state run liquor stores spend millions of dollars a year to promote drinking. However, across the street from them the government also established alcohol rehabilitation centers, both of which your tax dollars fund. What's wrong with this picture?

THE BIBLE, THE ONLY TRUTH AND NOTHING BUT THE TRUTH

Several years ago when I was preaching in the Leningrad Arena in the former United Soviet Socialist Republic, just after the back of communism was broken, I held up my Bible and said, "This is the Bible. It is the only Word of God." During that meeting, the Holy Spirit directed me to go back to America and preach that same word. Why? Because we have lost the hope of its message to humanism.

Marcus Borg, a Fellow of the Jesus Seminar, speaking at the United Methodist Seminar said, "We need to be clear and candid. The Bible is a human product. Ascribing it to divine inspiration leads to 'massive confusion.'"

God said through the prophet, Hosea, "I have written to him the great things of my law, but they were counted as a strange thing" (8:12).

Charles Haddon Spurgeon, the prince of preachers, said,

The Bible is the writing of the living God; each letter was penned with an Almighty finger; each word in it dropped from the everlasting lips; each sentence was dictated by the Holy Spirit. Moses was employed to record histories with his fiery pen guided by God. God moved David's hands over the living strings of his golden harp and let sweet Psalms of melody drop from his fingers. God directed the lips of Solomon, the preacher, and made him eloquent.

The Bible is like a vast roll of white linen, woven in the loom of truth; so you will have to continue unwinding it, roll after roll, before you get the real meaning of it from the very depth; and when you have found, as you think, a part of the meaning, you will still need to keep on unwinding, unwinding, and all eternity you will be unwinding the words of this wondrous volume.[8]

Another prophetic voice, A.W. Tozer, in his day said, "Whatever keeps me from the Bible is my enemy, however harmless it may appear to be. Whatever engages my attention when I should be meditating on God and things eternal does injury to my soul. Let the cares of life crowd out the Scriptures from my mind and I have suffered loss where I can least afford it. Let me accept anything else instead of the Scriptures and I have been cheated and robbed to my eternal confusion."[9]

There is no greater revelation than those found within the pages of our Bible. It is inspired, infallible and indivisible.

The Bible investigates subjects beyond human intellect —what man could have ever invented the grand doctrine of a Trinity in the Godhead; the sweet baptism of the Holy Ghost; redemption unto salvation; justification by faith; the communion of the saints; heaven to gain and hell to shun; a father who forgives the sinner but judges the rebellious; an everlasting citizenship in the new Jerusalem or, an everlasting banishment to an eternal burning hell?

It reveals the truth of the culmination of all things in one final battle as a prelude to Christ's grand processional to earth; that all things are ordered according to the will of one great Supreme Being, and work together for good.

It manifests motives, tries the spirits, tests the heart, exposes the sinner, convicts the Christian, dethrones doubt, forges faith, defeats death, glorifies God, crowns Christ and honors the Holy Spirit! Men have tried to burn it and bury it but it has always resurrected and beaten the pallbearers back to the house!

Congressman Tom DeLay said, "Our entire system is built on the Judeo-Christian ethic, but it fell apart when we started denying God. If you stand up today and acknowledge God, they will try to destroy you."

Congressman DeLay's main mission, he says, is "to bring us back to the Constitution and to the Absolute Truth that has been manipulated and destroyed by a liberal worldview."[10]

We need men and women who will once again agonize over the dying and destitute, raise the banner of the Bible and return the planks of doctrine to the Gospel bridge. We must again preach with power and purpose and we must pray with passion and pleading. We must solemnly preach and soberly proclaim ever stronger and ever louder the three R's—ruin, redemption and regeneration.

THE BLAME GAME

Today America is rolling in luxury, reveling in excess, rollicking in pleasure, revolting in morals and rotting in sin. What could you expect from a society in which passion is nothing more than riderless horses, where lust is exalted to lordship, sin is elevated to sovereignty, Satan is worshiped as a saint and man is magnified above His maker?

Accountability is made equal to being "judgmental." Holiness is rarely preached or expected. We promote peace and praise prosperity while our souls are poverty stricken and bankrupt. We have even become proficient at exploiting our plans and marketing our motives.

Another new wave of false doctrine is that of the politics of victimization. Since the beginning of time, humanity has played the most ancient of games: "the blame game." When Adam and Eve partook of the forbidden fruit, Adam attempted to blame Eve, "And the man said, The woman whom thou gavest to be with me, she gave me of the tree, and I did eat" (Genesis 3:12).

But look closely. He not only blamed Eve, he blamed God as well. For after all, He is the one who created Eve and gave her to the man! Adam was the first "victim."

It wasn't his fault that he sinned. Never mind that God had told him not to eat of the fruit of the tree of the knowledge of good and evil. Discard the fact that he was the one whom God placed in dominion to tend and keep the garden. Don't remind him that he walked in unbroken fellowship in the cool of the morning with the Most High God!

It was the woman and God who were to blame for his predicament. Had God not created Eve, then Adam would not have to take care of her. Adam was, I'm sure, too overworked anyway with all of His duties in the garden to keep track of what his rebellious wife was doing. He shouldn't have had to be responsible for her. After all, no one really wants responsibility because that brings accountability.

In the middle of paradise, Adam chose the archenemy of God in the greatest rebellion ever known to the human family. In the middle of all of this retrieval, man wound his moral clock backwards. The image of God had been dashed to pieces.

Man was driven with a flaming sword to the Eastern plains of sterile Eden. He stood in jeopardy before God and all of His holy angels and death was the mark on him. The only hope he had before him was the pit from whence he had been dug.

THE VICTIM SYNDROME

Today, within our society, there is a demonic undercurrent going on to try to blame everyone and everything else for our problems. Some excuses include: I am the wrong color, I was born on the wrong side of the tracks, I was poor, I was abused, I was this, I was that. However, no one wants to cite all of the wonderful opportunities God has given to us through His Word to be more than conquerers! Instead we have become victims of our own choosing. Consider the follow excerpt from the entitled, <u>A Nation of Victims</u>:

Portraying oneself as a victim has become an attractive pastime. . . . This rush to declare oneself a victim cannot be accounted for solely in political terms. Rather it suggests a more fundamental transformation of American cultural values and notions of character and personal responsibility.

A man who by his own admission has exposed himself between ten thousand and twenty thousand times (and been convicted of flashing on more than 30 occasions) is turned down for a job as a park attendant in Dane County, Wisconsin, because of his arrest record but sues on the grounds that he had never exposed himself in a park, only in libraries and laundromats. Wisconsin employment officials, ever accommodating to the expansion of human rights, agree and make "an initial determination of probable cause" that the flasher was the victim of illegal job discrimination.

As it becomes increasingly clear that misbehavior can be redefined as disease, growing numbers of the newly diseased have flocked to groups like Gamblers Anonymous, Pill Addicts Anonymous, S-Anon ("relatives and friends of sex addicts"), Nicotine Anonymous, Youth Emotions Anonymous, Unwed Parents Anonymous, Emotional Health Anonymous, Debtors Anonymous, Workaholics Anonymous, Dual Disorders Anonymous, Batterers Anonymous, Victims Anonymous, and Families of Sex Offenders Anonymous.

Something extraordinary is happening in American society. Crisscrossed by invisible trip wires of emotional, racial, sexual, and psychological griev-ance, American life is increasingly characterized by the plaintive insistence, *I am a victim.* The mantra of the victims is the same: *I am not responsible; it's not my fault.*[11]

The church has failed to become the hospital for a dying world bleeding to death by the injuries it has caused itself. We have attempted to put a Band-Aid® on the open sore of sin as it continues to become infected just below the surface.

The Bible says, "Behold, all souls are mine; as the soul of the father, so also the soul of the son is mine: the soul that sinneth, it shall die. But if a man be just, and do that which is lawful and right" (Ezekiel 18:4,5). You and I are still responsible for our own actions!

However, four thousand years earlier, when Adam and Eve revolted against God, He laid out a plan to return us to Himself. He gave us a propitiation . . . He promised a sacri-fice with hope.

It was not a foliage sacrifice. It was not payment for just some iniquity. Our high priest, Jesus, left eternity's majesty for an earthly manger, and He has come to repair, reconcile and restore the relationship between a timeless God and a temporal man.

There is a hope through Jesus Christ. God help us to return to our past, so that we can live holy in the present and experience revival!

Chapter Eleven

Return God to Our Educational System

Billy Sunday, a professional baseball player turned preacher, once said, "I say, with Waite of Colorado, that the rivers of America will run with blood filled to their banks before we will submit to them taking the Bible out of our schools."

Instead of heeding the words of Sunday, the church chose to sleep like grasshoppers and then panic in a crisis. Little did either know that in 1962 prayer in school would be banned and the vast majority of the church would slowly but freely begin to hand over their religious freedoms. The sixth key to bringing America and the church back to Jesus Christ is to return God to our educational system. The Bible records:

> And the king went up into the house of the Lord, and all the men of Judah, and the inhabitants of Jerusalem, and the priests, and the Levites, and all the people, great and small: and he read in their ears

all the words of the book of the covenant that was found in the house of the Lord.

And the king stood in his place, and made a covenant before the Lord, to walk after the Lord, and to keep his commandments, and his testimonies, and his statutes, with all his heart, and with all his soul, to perform the words of the covenant which are written in this book (2 Chronicles 34:30,31).

Could it be that we could have a president who would unburden parents from the pressure of making sure their children are taught at least some semblance of moral values?

LEAVING THE HOUSE OF BREAD

Most are familiar with the story of Ruth, a Moabite in the Old Testament, whose husband died. This young woman returned with her mother-in-law, Naomi, to live in her homeland and later married Boaz and became an ancestor of Jesus Christ.

But the beginning of this story is not so hopeful. It is about Naomi's husband, Elimelech, who took his family in the midst of famine and left for another town.

Now it came to pass in the days when the judges ruled, that there was a famine in the land. And a certain man of Bethlehemjudah went to sojourn in the country of Moab, he, and his wife, and his two sons.

And the name of the man was Elimelech, and the name of his wife Naomi, and the name of his two sons Mahlon and Chilion, Ephrathites of Bethlehemjudah. And they came into the country of Moab, and continued there.

And Elimelech Naomi's husband died; and she was left, and her two sons. And they took them wives of the women of Moab; the name of the one was Orpah, and the name of the other Ruth: and they dwelled there about ten years.

And Mahlon and Chilion died also both of them; and the woman was left of her two sons and her husband (Ruth 1:1-5).

Death had caused this family to turn dark with tragedy. Their tears flowed like a river at the loss of fathers, sons and husbands.

The Bible is very specific in pointing out to us that there was a systematic progression to what happened to Elimelech and his family. These were people of great substance. As the book of Ruth relates, they came into the country of Moab and Elimelech, Naomi's husband, died. There is no further description of this man apart from that he died and his two sons as well.

This story is ripe with information, prophetically, to where you and I are living today. The book of Ruth in this first chapter is dealing with a time when the judges ruled. It was actually at the very beginning of the judges' authority in

Israel. Their authority was not a national authority, but rather a local authority which lent itself to a lot of schisms and division and infighting and uprising.

This time in history held its place between the death of Joshua, who had led them across Jordan in three days time to inhabit the promised land in 31 conquests, and the beginning of the rule of kings in Israel. Victory was on every hand. Israel possessed the land, and they were living in the land that God promised them. They had come out of the wandering, howling, screaming wilderness, and now they were standing full well in the place of promise.

In fact, this story takes place with a man who lived in Bethlehem, which could be referred to as the house of bread or the house of praise. Bethlehem, by name, means God's house. It was the doorway into the presence of the Almighty, where the covering, brooding Spirit of God stretched out a protective haven over them that was impenetrable by the forces of darkness.

But now, Elimelech and his family were living in a time of darkness and tragedy. Like our day, it was a time of political, moral, social, and spiritual chaos. Everything was in a turmoil.

This was a time characterized by several conditions. First of all, there was the condition of hostile intrusion. Judges were in positions of authority, but they were factious. They were separated from their parts. There was division and infighting among them which made them and those they ruled accessible to the forces of darkness.

God sends us the Holy Spirit to seal us (or protect us), to keep that which is on the outside from getting in. When my mother used to can fruits and vegetables at home and cut coupons just to make ends meet, to take care of my sister and me, no one said it would be easy. You can't give your child an opportunity to be reared in the "house of bread" when there is no protective covering over your children.

We've become so weak, anemic, self-satisfied and self-indulgent that we are sacrificing the future of the church and the eternity of our children on the altars of our own pleasure.

There are many who are saved today so much so that the numbers are almost too great to comprehend. However, it is entirely possible for someone to have a saved life, a saved soul and a lost life. This is what Elimelech experienced.

INVASION OF LIFE AS WE KNOW IT

When I began to study these five verses of Scripture in Ruth, the Holy Spirit spoke to me and said, "Tell America their homes are being invaded. Tell them the minds of their children are being invaded. While they sit in Sunday morning service and go through the motions and read the Bible every now and then, their children's minds are being invaded. Their spirits are being invaded, because they have thrust them into a situation where they are surrounded with the inhabitants of Moab."

There is light, and there is darkness. There is saved, and there is lost. The Lord has given us the responsibility to protect our children, our righteous seed. The Bible says, "Lo, children are an heritage of the Lord: and the fruit of the womb is his reward" (Psalm 127:3).

The hour is critical in which we must rise up with a righteous indignation and say, "My children are the heritage of the Lord!"

Paul declared to the church at Corinth, "Be ye not unequally yoked together with unbelievers: for what fellowship hath righteousness with unrighteousness? and what communion hath light with darkness? Wherefore come out from among them, and be ye separate, saith the Lord, and touch not the unclean thing; and I will receive you" (2 Corinthians 6:14,17).

Americans' homes, minds, and their children's minds are being invaded constantly. If not used properly, demonic forces can encroach on our homes through the internet, television, radio, magazines, and other various forms of media.

What kind of parent allows their child to sit for hours at a time unattended at a computer? We need to understand that we are being invaded. There's an invasion of darkness, pain and the spirit of the world. It is not only coming through the internet, television and printed material, but it is also coming through the songs our children listen to.

Our children are being inundated with foul, violent and lewd lyrics pawned off as artistic expression while the music industry lines their pockets with our children's money. Songs which encourage rape, incest, murder, racism and rebellion can be found in CD players across the country. Proverb 4:23 warns us against what we allow ourselves and our children to listen to, "Above all else, guard your affections. For they influence everything else in your life" (TLB).

It is a time of hostile intrusion into the hearts of our children. While the nuclear home is exploding by leaps and bounds, the traditional family is slowly disintegrating all around us.

Children require an investment of time and are considered more of a financial responsibility than anyone would care to admit. Thus, they are sacrificed on the altar of self-gratification. Don't ask parents to sacrifice their careers or costly homes or expensive cars for the unimaginable opportunity to nurture and care for a child.

When children are present, most often they are treated as another pet equal to a dog or cat that can be loved and attended to only when it is convenient for the parent. Therefore, the minds of our righteous seed are being turned toward the world because we have dysfunctional homes and churches. No wonder they develop worldly appetites when it appears their schools and friends have more to offer than we do.

WHAT ARE THE PARENTS' RIGHTS?

But what kind of spirit is our educational system putting into our children? When the pilgrims settled at Plymouth Rock, their greatest desire was to educate their children so that they could read the Bible for themselves. Today, however, the paradigm has greatly shifted. Instead of teaching moral decency and the Bible as the bedrock for all other truth, our children are flooded with everything but a solid, God-based curricula. Ponder the following excerpt from *The Assault on Parenthood:*

Most parents regret the passing of a time when order

reigned in the classroom, and what you got from schools was, if not an intellectually rigorous education, at least a core curriculum directed toward functional literacy.

Our schools have changed—and for the worse, parents say. All over the country parents fret over the increase in school violence and classroom misbehavior.

Parents consistently lament the failure of the schools to turn out productive citizens who can read, write, or perform the simplest arithmetic. Have children forgotten how to learn? No, insist parents. Behind the failures of many an American child are schools that have forgotten how to teach.

Less than 60% of American 17 year olds could figure out simple percentages and over 60% of adults in their 20s could not articulate the major argument of a newspaper article.

The late 1980s revealed that one-third of American high school seniors did not know who wrote the Emancipation Proclamation, and that two-thirds could not place the Civil War within half a century. No more than one-third of high school seniors are "proficient readers," a decline of 10% between the years 1992 and 1994 alone.

Why does the American educational system produce such sorry results? One reason, parents say, is that the schools have confused their mission. A mother observes: "My 8th grade son came home the other day and said they had discussed sexual foreplay in his 'L.I.F.E.' class. Now he knows how to get it on with a girl at a party. What he doesn't know is what a preposition is. For that, I have to hire an English tutor at $50 an hour."

The overriding educational philosophy promoted in schools is that the major function of school is to make children "feel good about themselves."

Schools [intend to] reshape values, attitudes and beliefs to fit a very different vision of the world from what children have received from their parents. Educators have a specific set of goals in this respect: to discomfit children about the security of the world around them; to break down their reserve, discretion, and sense of privacy; to discredit their faith in parental goodwill and authority; and to assault the traditional values children learn at home and at church. "Parents who send their children to school with instructions to respect and obey their teachers," Thomas Sowell warns, "may be surprised to discover how often these children are sent back home conditioned to disrespect and disobey their parents."[1]

THE REWRITING OF HISTORY

The statistics bear out that we need a heartfelt revival in our educational system. Note that history classes are now being taught from a "contemporary view of history." History, itself, has been rewritten to conform to the liberal ideology so prevalent in our schools today. This insidious process has been undermining our students' ability to grasp and know the truth of our nation's formation.

Heroes, such as Thomas Jefferson, George Washington, and others who fought to give us the liberties we hold so dear are also depreciated by making them equal to such tyrants as Mao Tse Tung, Adolf Hitler and Joseph Stalin. The result has been a mass exodus from patriotism and military service. Study the following statistics and you will begin to understand what the end conclusion is:

Almost a quarter of America's teenagers have trouble passing a fourth-grade level U.S. history test, according to a recent survey commissioned by the Colonial Williamsburg Foundation. In fact, 22 percent could not name the country from which the United States declared its independence, with 14 percent thinking that "France" was the correct answer.

The study in which 1000 teenagers nationwide were surveyed, also revealed that 17 percent did not know there were 13 original colonies, and that 15 percent were unaware that the Continental Congress adopted the Declaration of Independence on July 4, 1776. Among the other findings in the survey:

1. Twenty-four percent did not know who fought in the Civil War, 13 percent thinking it was the United States and Great Britain.

2. Nineteen percent could not identify the three branches of government.

3. Thirty-one percent did not know who wrote "The Star Spangled Banner."[2]

There is some hope, however, when in June 2000 an amendment to the Senate education bill introduced by Senator Rick Santorum (R-Pa.) passed. It stated that "schools should teach students 'to distinguish the data or testable theories of science from philosophical or religious claims that are made in the name of science.'"[3]

President Bush has also promised to help parents with children in failing schools through the possibility of school vouchers. As of this writing, intense pressure has mounted to stop such intervention in the education of our children and this issue is quickly losing ground. What must we do to halt the trend toward a godless, dumbed-down educational system?

ORDER IN THE CLASSROOM

Elimelech's days represented a time of heresy when the

world looked better than the church and God was banished from the lives of men. The people had heard the words of the law given to Moses. They just didn't adhere to them.

The consequence was his children lost respect for the preacher. They saw him as nothing more than a raving madman. They thought his ideas were obsolete. They determined in their mind that they knew better. After all, he just didn't understand their situation.

Thus, prayer, never mind school prayer, has become a relic of the past. Even student-led prayers during high school graduation ceremonies have been labeled divisive. In a recent case, a valedictorian student filed a lawsuit to stop student-led prayer during her Washington High School commencement. A sympathetic class president stated before the school board:

> To say that there is a deity is sowing seeds of intolerance and divisiveness throughout the senior class, especially for those who believe in multiple gods or no god at all. Step aside from your personal views and look at diversity.

> After issuing a restraining order to halt the prayers, Judge Joe Billy McDade said, "If one student at Washington Community High School is deprived of his or her constitutional rights, then that takes precedence over the rights of the majority."[4]

A poll indicated that an astonishing 77 percent were opposed to the ban on prayer. Oddly, in the end there was more prayer offered for this particular commencement than in the entire 80 years of the school's history.

We need to restore order to the classroom and halls of our schools again. However, first we must restore order to our own personal lives as Christians.

LAWLESSNESS RULES

The generation of today is similar to Elimelech's generation because they were also inundated with lawlessness. This lawlessness was not necessarily directed toward the law of the land (though that can be an outgrowth) but the law of God. This anarchy can be found through the continuing rise of sexual promiscuity and drug and alcohol abuse among our teenagers.

For instance, HIV infection among teenage girls has risen at an alarming rate of 117% from heterosexual sex between the years 1994 and 1998.[5]

In the Spring of 2001, the International Planned Parenthood Foundation, the largest abortion proponent and provider in the world, published a new Youth Manifesto. It's premise is to communicate to young people that sex is fun and should be encouraged. It encourages the unholy practice outside of the God-ordained confines of marriage.[6]

Drug use among school-aged children continues to skyrocket. A current survey said that "more than two in five U.S. high school seniors have used an illegal drug such as marijuana or steroids during the 2000-2001 academic year."[7]

Our schools are also peddling homosexuality as an alternative lifestyle which should not be condoned nor encouraged. Take, for instance, in October 2000, the National Education Association (NEA) President Bob Chase gave parents a cause for alarm when he pledged his support to homosexual activists in advancing the gay agenda in schools. Touted as the "New B" Resolution, it would promote homosexuality as an acceptable lifestyle among adolescents and adults alike in our nation's classrooms.

The "New B" resolution would promote this obscene lifestyle in the following ways:

1. Implement pro-gay instructional materials in classrooms, kindergarten through 12th grade;

2. Encourage gay teachers to be role models in their schools;

3. Encourage districts to hire homosexual teachers and

4. Encourage schools to work with gay activist organizations to promote and develop gay-friendly curricula.[8]

In essence, every course in the public school system would be fair game for advancing the gay agenda. Opposition within the ranks of the NEA as well as from parents nationally, has stagnated the pro-homosexuals plan to rewrite curricula to accommodate this sinful practice.

Though any decision on the "New B" resolution has been delayed, do not be deceived into believing that it is dead. Dr. James Dobson shared the potential of such passage of this crucial decision.

> In Marin County, California, all second graders through-fifth graders at Pleasant Valley School were called to an assembly put on by a local theater group without the parents' permission, Dobson said. 'The group taught the children slogans such as, 'I'm Gay; it's okay.'"

> Dobson related that a fourth-grade child went home after the assembly and told his parents he learned about families with two daddies and two mommies and words like "homosexual" and "lesbian." A third-grade girl, meanwhile repeatedly asked her father if she was a lesbian because she like girls better than boys.[9]

Now is not the time to sit back and relax as our children die in Moab! Homosexual activism, though a minority group, is on the rise. Why? Because there is no shame for their sin. The Bible very clearly says, "The very look on their faces gives them away and shows their guilt. And they boast that their sin is equal to the sin of Sodom; they are not even ashamed. What a catastrophe! They have doomed themselves" (Isaiah 3:9 TLB).

What will it take to set America and the world's children on course again? A true revival by returning God to our educational system!

FAMINE IN THE LAND

Another characteristic during the times Elimelech lived were that the people of God had experienced famine in the land. Famine, as you may know, is the result of no rain.

During spiritual famine, the heavens are shut off by idolatry. Elimelech was running away from a national problem that sprang from individual roots.

What was Elimelech's problem? He was only interested in how the whole could serve him, with no interest in how he could serve the whole. In other words, he complained about a problem of which he was a primary root. Instead of staying in Bethlehem and letting God use him, he chose the coward's way out. He took his family and ran. Instead of becoming a part of fixing the problem, which Elimelech helped create, his response was to abandon the House of Bread.

Elimelech exaggerated the problem. Out of all the nation of Israel, he and his family were the only ones who chose to leave. The famine was not so great as to warrant him leaving. Allow me to pose this question, "How are you going to die of famine in the house of bread?"

Elimelech's problem was that he faced some hard times. Everything didn't pop up posies for him and his boys. So instead of toughing it out, waiting on the blessing and for things to get better, he abandoned ship. By so doing, he set a poor example to everybody else, and especially his family.

Elimelech weakened the hands of his brethren when he should have been fighting with them against the plight of famine. Matthew Henry, one of the greatest Bible scholars and commentators said it this way:

It is an evidence of a discontented, distrustful, unstable spirit, to be weary of the place in which God hath set us, and to be for leaving it immediately whenever we meet with any uneasiness or inconvenience in it. It is folly to think of escaping that cross which, being laid in our way, we ought to take up. It is our wisdom to make the best of that which is, for it is seldom that changing our place is mending it.[10]

Elimelech died, and I would venture to say that he went to heaven. But because times became troubled, he sought escape. Most noteworthy is that he sought it away from the protective covering of God. He exposed his children to an exotic, sinful and alluring environment.

Abraham raised his children to know God. Elimelech raised his children to know the world. He took them to Moab, left them there and lost them there.

Do you know what one of the saddest things is? You would have thought that when Elimelech died his sons would have said, "Our father always talked about getting back home to Bethlehem. We should not bury him in Moab, instead we should go back to Canaan." However, for whatever reason they used to justify their decision, they chose to stay and dwell in the land of Moab.

Elimelech's sons died at a young age because they were out from under the protective covering of God. Elimelech was more concerned that they have prestige in the eyes of the world than that they be known in the courts of heaven.

Remember, Lot's wife. She longed for Sodom more than her salvation. As a result, she did what she shouldn't have done and looked upon what she should not have seen. The book of Genesis states, "And it came to pass, when they had brought them forth abroad, that he said, Escape for thy life; look not behind thee, neither stay thou in all the plain; escape to the mountain, lest thou be consumed. But his wife looked back from behind him, and she became a pillar of salt. (19:17, 26)"

The church must quit looking back to the glitter and the allure of the world. Instead we must stay steadfast and set our affections on things above. We cannot allow anything to detour us or our children from our destiny. We must do as the Apostle Paul did, "Brethren, I count not myself to have apprehended: but this one thing I do, forgetting those things which are behind, and reaching forth unto those things which are before, I press toward the mark for the prize of the high calling of God in Christ Jesus" (Philippians 3:13,14).

I am on a campaign to save the lives of children in this nation. God is calling us to shut the door on the invasionary forces of darkness which are trying to get a foothold in our lives and families. Let us stand up for holiness and godliness. Let us make the declaration, "The world has nothing for me or my family! I determine to take a stand and see revival come to my home and my children's school!"

Chapter Twelve

Rebuild Our Altars

Former President Theodore Roosevelt once said, "The true Christian is the true citizen, lofty of purpose, resolute in endeavor, ready for a hero's deeds, but never looking down on his task because it is cast in the day of small things; scornful of baseness, awake to his own duties as well as to his rights, following the higher law of reverence, and in this world doing all that in his power lies, so that when death comes he may feel that mankind is in some degree better because he lived."[1]

As Christians and citizens, the last and most important thing that we must do is to rebuild both our personal and family altars. Therefore, we must have a return to the atonement. Moreover, we must have a renaissance of its four major characteristics, which include salvation, healing, deliverance, and prosperity. When you see these things working together, there will be a national revival.

During Josiah's reign, in an act of repentance and

restoration, he prepared the biggest Passover in all the history of the kings of Israel and Judah and set the example for what we must now do to rebuild our altars.

Moreover Josiah kept a passover unto the Lord in Jerusalem: and they killed the passover on the fourteenth day of the first month. And he set the priests in their charges, and encouraged them to the service of the house of the Lord, And said unto the Levites that taught all Israel, which were holy unto the Lord, Put the holy ark in the house which Solomon the son of David king of Israel did build; it shall not be a burden upon your shoulders: serve now the Lord your God, and his people Israel.

And prepare yourselves by the houses of your fathers, after your courses, according to the writing of David king of Israel, and according to the writing of Solomon his son.

So all the service of the Lord was prepared the same day, to keep the passover, and to offer burnt offerings upon the altar of the Lord, according to the commandment of king Josiah.

And the children of Israel that were present kept the passover at that time, and the feast of unleavened bread seven days.

And there was no passover like to that kept in Israel

from the days of Samuel the prophet; neither did all the kings of Israel keep such a passover as Josiah kept, and the priests, and the Levites, and all Judah and Israel that were present, and the inhabitants of Jerusalem (2 Chronicles 35:1-4, 16-18).

A great feast was made for the passover and the ark was brought again to its holy place. This does not necessarily refer to the physical movement of the ark but of setting the Word of God back upon the throne of our hearts. The result is a repair in the breach of our lives, families and country. It is a restoration of the paths to dwell in. (See Isaiah 58:12.)

ATONEMENT BRINGS RESTORATION

In the Old Testament, in an effort to restore the people to God temporarily, an atonement for sins was to be made. This was what Josiah enacted during the passover. Leviticus 25 chronicles these words,

And the Lord spake unto Moses in mount Sinai, saying, Speak unto the children of Israel, and say unto them, When ye come into the land which I give you, then shall the land keep a sabbath unto the Lord. Six years thou shalt sow thy field, and six years thou shalt prune thy vineyard, and gather in the fruit thereof; But in the seventh year shall be a sabbath of rest unto the land, a sabbath for the Lord: thou shalt neither sow thy field, nor prune thy vineyard.

And thou shalt number seven sabbaths of years unto thee, seven times seven years; and the space of the seven sabbaths of years shall be unto thee forty and nine years. Then shalt thou cause the trumpet of the jubile to sound on the tenth day of the seventh month, in the day of atonement shall ye make the trumpet sound throughout all your land (vv. 1-4, 8,9).

In this passage of Scripture, the children of Israel were getting ready to celebrate the Day of Atonement. The word atonement can be divided into three parts, at-one-ment, to mean a reconciliation between humanity and God Almighty.

The high priest, on the Day of Atonement would slay fifteen beasts, wash himself five times, and could receive no help from any of the other priests. He had to offer the sacrifice alone for the atonement of Israel's sins. The blood from the slain animals ran like a crimson, red stream, historians tell us, 24 hours a day.

Atonement also means redemption. Redemption is God's way, through the blood of Jesus, to return man to his original state of affairs—that is as when Adam first walked with God in the Garden of Eden before he sinned. After this act of high treason, God prepared a plan where 4000 years later the temporary covering wrought by the blood from the sacrifice of animals would no longer be needed.

Religion has and will always be the attempt of humanity to reach God. However, Christianity in its purest form is God condescending to humanity. We did not "find the Lord," for we did not even know where to look for Him.

Rather, it was God who sought for Moses and found him at Midian. It was Jehovah who looked for Jacob and found him at Bethel. It was the Lord who looked for Saul and found him on the road to Damascus. Today, this same God has come in search of a people whom He can use to turn this world upside down!

JESUS OUR ATONEMENT

Everything that was involved in the Old Testament Day of Atonement—the priesthood, old covenants, altars, and sacrifices—were done away with. God rendered it void and of no effect with the arrival of His Son, Jesus, upon the earth.

In the Old Testament, the Israelites were required to offer a lamb for their house as an atonement for their sins. Jesus became the new sacrifice, the Lamb of God which takes away the sins of the world. God also established a new, eternal altar in heaven where Jesus lives to intercede for believers.

Without the blood of Jesus, baptism means nothing. Without the blood, liturgy means nothing. Without the blood, catechism means nothing. Without the blood, church attendance, good works and Bible reading mean nothing. Why? Because the Bible says, "For Christ sent me not to baptize, but to preach the gospel: not with wisdom of words, lest the cross of Christ should be made of none effect. For the preaching of the cross is to them that perish foolishness; but unto us which are saved it is the power of God" (1 Corinthians 1:17,18).

Our Lord and Savior, Jesus Christ, was crucified on the Day of Atonement when God's people were trying to stay the hand of judgment. In ancient Israel, everyone gathered at Jerusalem on Mount Moriah to bring sacrifices for their families. The blood from their sacrifices flowed down through the Kidron Valley, into the Virgin's Fount, and, ultimately, into the Dead Sea just outside the ancient city. On Golgatha's hillside, the Lamb of God hung on an old, rugged cruel beam, and became the sacrifice for humanity who took away the sins of the world.

We are people of immediacy. We are people of the temporal. We are people of the right now. How then can we allow ourselves to think about tomorrow, two months or even two years from now, much less to think with an eternal perspective?

There has developed in the church a tendency to look back over our shoulder at the world from which we came. We need a new perspective.

Jesus said, "For whosoever will save his life shall lose it: but whosoever will lose his life for my sake, the same shall save it" (Luke 9:24). Your life is not your own.

The Bible is very specific in declaring, "There is a way which seemeth right unto a man, but the end thereof are the ways of death" (Proverb 14:12).

Christ's sphere of conflict was the Cross of Calvary. There He came in crowning glory, a Conqueror whose conquest was branded upon a wooden post by the blood which trickled down its splintered side into a pool at the base of the tree. This was a picture forever frozen in time—the day the earth stood still and the angels dared not sing heaven's sweet song.

Jesus became the sacrificial Lamb, taking within His

body not just one sin, one lie, one malicious thought but all the sins of humanity. He bore every sin—past, present and future.

Imagine, if you will, the tentacles of Satan's terrorists tearing at the Savior's flesh. Allow your mind to envision a portrait of principalities whose fangs have been dipped in the poison of sin.

Every bondage, infirmity, malady and malfunction hastened in hordes to do battle with Him on the Cross. Jesus took upon Himself, in His body, all your sin, every one that you committed or ever will commit! It was Jesus against the world!

Colossians 2:15 says, "And having spoiled principalities and powers, he made a shew of them openly, triumphing over them in it." Then crying from the very depths of His Spirit, Jesus declared, "It is finished!"

Grace was birthed at the foot of His Cross. John 1:16,17 announces, "And of his fulness have all we received, and grace for grace. For the law was given by Moses, but grace and truth came by Jesus Christ."

Jesus then descended into the depths of the doomed and the damned to reclaim everything the devil had stolen. Ephesians 4:8 declares: "The Psalmist tells about this, for he says that when Christ returned triumphantly to heaven after his resurrection and victory over Satan, he gave generous gifts to men" (TLB).

The voice of mercy could be heard calling through the corridors of hell. Jesus divided the spoil that had long been chained to the chariot of our archenemy, Lucifer, the Prince of Lies.

Jesus took your children, money, deliverance, and healing from the clutches of Satan. He spent three days taking back what rightfully belongs to you!

Our Conquering Canaan King took the yoke that was meant for your neck and put it upon Satan's neck. Then the prophetic words of Isaiah became forever sealed in history, "And it shall come to pass in that day, that his burden shall be taken away from off thy shoulder, and his yoke from off thy neck, and the yoke shall be destroyed because of the anointing." (10:27).

Christ led a crowning processional through the corridors of hell past the forever mountain to the gates of the Celestial City. There our King of kings made a show of Satan openly. This is what the Lord of Glory did for you and me.

The Bible says that our great High Priest is even now at the right hand of the Father making intercession for us. (See Romans 8:34.) Therefore, when Satan begins to accuse you, answer, "Who shall lay anything to the charge of God's elect?"

If you sin, 1 John 2:1 states, "My little children, these things write I unto you, that ye sin not. And if any man sin, we have an advocate [the Amplified Bible says, "One Who will intercede for us"] with the Father, Jesus Christ the righteous."

My sin, not just in part but the whole has been nailed to His Cross. To those blackmailed by sin, Jesus, in an act of jubilant defiance, erased the allusion of eternal allegiance to the alien armies of our adversary.

ATONEMENT BRINGS HEALING AND DELIVERANCE

The lambs and goats that were sacrificed during Josiah's time could only provide a temporary solution for the eternal problem of sin. However, when Jesus spilled His blood on Calvary, the price was paid in full not only for your salvation, but also for your healing and deliverance. Did you know that the three most commonly asked questions regarding healing are: "Will God heal me?" "Can God heal me?" and "Is it God's will for me to be healed?" But as a child of God you have the right to walk in His healing power.

How do you appropriate God's healing power? You do so by speaking His Word and allowing it to sink deep within your spirit. Romans 10:17 declares, "So then faith cometh by hearing, and hearing by the word of God."

The power of declaring God's Word is so important to your healing. Your words speak volumes into the spirit realm. As you begin to declare, by the words of your mouth, how it shall be, like a light turned on in a dark room, the Word of God becomes larger than life on the inside of you. Scripture verses such as, "Who his own self bare our sins in his own body on the tree, that we, being dead to sins, should live unto righteousness: by whose stripes ye were healed" (1 Peter 2:24) become revelation knowledge.

Like a surgical instrument, God begins to remove the pain and disease invading your body. Through the filter of His blood, Jesus, our Great Physician, begins to treat the symptoms of your sickness.

On the backside of Calvary, between Christ and the

Cross, the miraculous began. Jesus' wound flowed against the bark of the tree. A crimson stain marked the post, thereby initiating God's redeeming Passover of man's sickness.

The Bible still declares, that today is the day of salvation and now is the appointed time. (See 2 Corinthians 6:2.) Salvation means healing, deliverance, prosperity—whatever you need!

The Lord will honor His Word . . . He always does. He put so much at stake in His Word that the Psalmist made this declaration, "I will worship toward thy holy temple, and praise thy name for thy lovingkindness and for thy truth: for thou hast magnified thy word above all thy name" (Psalm 138:2).

Jesus Christ, the Anointed One, wants to remove calamity, malady and malfunction from your life. You are the tabernacle of His healing power; therefore, you can receive His healing power even now.

WE NEED GOD'S PRESENCE AND POWER FOR THIS REVIVAL

Jesus is greater than He has been preached. That is why this key is so integral to revival. He destroyed the power of sin, sickness, disease and poverty. We need to rebuild the altars of Holy Ghost baptism.

We need the One who promised to come and indwell mortals, to come even now and fill us full of Himself.

When the power of Jesus Christ comes upon us, it will cause us to tread upon serpents and scorpions and dance as we go. This power will enable us to walk through the fire and its flames will not kindle upon us. This power will enable us to pass through the flood, and it not overflow us. It is Holy Ghost power!

Acts 1:8 says, "But ye shall receive power, after that the Holy Ghost is come upon you: and ye shall be witnesses unto me both in Jerusalem, and in all Judaea, and in Samaria, and unto the uttermost part of the earth."

What have we been given power over? Jesus gave us power over depravity, disease, deception, and the devil.

When you receive this power which is available to you through the baptism of the Holy Spirit, the Bible declares, He that is with you shall be in you. (See John 14:17.) And, "Greater is he that is in you, than he that is in the world" (1 John 4:4). God can initiate a revival through your words, through your hands and through your life!

TIMES OF REFRESHING

There is a wind starting to blow. God is ready to restore and refresh the body of Christ. This Scripture promises that once repentance is completed, God will refresh us with a fresh wind of His presence.

Acts 3:19 says, "Repent ye therefore, and be converted,that your sins may be blotted out, when the times of refreshing shall come fro the presence of the Lord."

Oh, how we need God's presence. We have sacrificed His presence for His power. We have used Him as our escape from problems and persecution and then cast Him aside until our next crisis. We need Him more than we need our next breath!

I believe God is preparing to send His people the refreshing, restoring presence of the Holy Spirit which will usher in this great revival.

The Lord wants to restore and refresh your life so "he might present . . . a glorious church, not having spot, or wrinkle, or any such thing; but that it should be holy and without blemish" (Ephesians 5:27). He is in the process of pulling you and me out of this world.

Today, you and I live in a society where right has been wrong for so long that righteousness has now become the abnormal thing. God is calling the body of Christ to be different. He is calling us to rise far above the moral climate of our day. He wants us to rebuild our altars and become a "living sacrifice, holy, acceptable unto Him, which is our reasonable service. And be not conformed to this world: but be ye transformed by the renewing of your mind, that ye may prove what is that good, and acceptable, and perfect, will of God" (Romans 12:1b,2).

This is what God wants for you. This is the refreshing and restoring He wants to send your way. However, God is not looking for an "ordinary" church. Instead, I believe He longs to surgically extract from your innermost being any contentment with church as normal.

REBUILD OUR PERSONAL AND FAMILY ALTARS

Remembering George Whitefield and the effect his

preaching had on the colonies and their families, Benjamin Franklin said, "It was wonderful to see the change soon made in the manners of our inhabitants. From being thoughtless or indifferent about religion, it seemed as if all the world were growing religious, so that one could not walk thro' the town in an evening without hearing psalms sung in different families of every street."[2]

Revival begins in the heart of the believer, and then makes its way through their family, neighborhood, town, city and state until it has traversed to the outer limits of the world.

Therefore, we must rebuild the altars of our hearts so that they are fit for the King we claim to serve. We need to remember that it is He who gave us the power to overcome, through the blood of Jesus, any and every obstacle that may stand in our way. We must not and cannot forget the Lord, our God, because the Bible has this ominous warning, "The wicked shall be turned into hell, and all the nations that forget God" (Psalm 9:17).

On December 22, 1820, Daniel Webster reminded those gathered at the Bicentennial Celebration of the landing of the Pilgrims at Plymouth Rock, Massachusetts:

Finally, let us not forget the religious character of our origin. Our fathers were brought hither by their high veneration for the Christian religion. They journeyed by its light, and labored in its hope. They sought to incorporate its principles with the elements of their society, and to diffuse its influence through all their institutions, civil, political, or literary.

Let us cherish these sentiments, and extend this influence still more widely; in full conviction that is the happiest society which partakes in the highest degree of the mild and peaceful spirit of Christianity. [Plymouth was] the spot where the first scene of our history was laid; where the hearth and altars of new England were placed, where Christianity, and civilization, and letters made their first lodgement, in a vast extent of country.[3]

It is time to tear down the altars which have long been used to offer up the sacrifices of our own lust. We cannot delay another day.

In order to rebuild our personal and family altars, there comes a time when our God, known as Elohim, the God of creation, the God of heaven and earth, must become Adonai to us, the Lord of our lives. There comes an hour when it is all or nothing for the Lord.

There comes a point in each of our lives when two roads diverge before us and we must choose which one to take. Near to the time of his death, Joshua proclaimed,

Now therefore fear the Lord, and serve him in sincerity and in truth: and put away the gods which your fathers served on the other side of the flood, and in Egypt; and serve ye the Lord.

And if it seem evil unto you to serve the Lord, choose you this day whom ye will serve; whether the gods which your fathers served that were on the other side of the flood, or the gods of the Amorites, in whose land ye dwell: but as for me and my house, we will serve the Lord (Joshua 24:14,15).

That choice can only be made at the altar of the heart. There we must solemnly bow our head and humbly declare, "Lord, here is my life, my fortune, my family, my friends, my influence. Take out of me the desire for anything in the world and anything outside the bounds of your kingdom. Revive me again!"

Epilogue

Are We Ready to Respond?

At the close of the Twentieth Century the world waited and watched to see if Y2K and the emergence of a new millennium would be the tell-tale sign and factor to usher in the return of Jesus Christ prophesied by so many.

Would we be overrun with computer failures? Would nuclear war be imminent because of glitches in the mechanisms designed to avert any unrealistic threats? Would airplanes veer off course because of technical difficulties caused by the so-called Y2K bug?

As the clock on December 31, 1999 struck midnight, the world stood seemingly still. What would happen to life as we knew it?

Midnight came and went. When chaos seemed inevitable, only calm ensued. Throughout the earth another disaster was again diverted. The world continued on eating, drinking, and making merry.

But the clock keeps ticking.

Jesus issued this ominous warning to His disciples,

But of that day and hour knoweth no man, no, not the angels of heaven, but my Father only. But as the days of Noe were, so shall also the coming of the Son of man be. For as in the days that were before the flood they were eating and drinking, marrying and giving in marriage, until the day that Noe entered into the ark, And knew not until the flood came, and took them all away; so shall also the coming of the Son of man be (Matthew 24:36-39).

How long can we breathe a sigh of relief and continue with our current heart's condition? How long can we divert danger from a world on the pathway to an eternity lost without God? How can we anticipate Christ's return when Jesus, Himself, clearly said that no one knows the hour, only the Father in heaven?

At the beginning of this book, I shared briefly about the Doomsday Clock and its measure of the potential of a nuclear holocaust. Fifteen times the world was frozen by a conceivable crisis, fifteen times the crisis was averted.

Will it take another crisis to call us to our knees? I pray not. Will it take persecution and oppression from without to change the body of Christ from within? Possibly.

The parable of the ten virgins is a prime example of the necessity for preparation for this end-time age—in order to witness a revival spoken of but yet to be experienced.

Then shall the kingdom of heaven be likened unto ten virgins, which took their lamps, and went forth to meet the bridegroom. And five of them were wise, and five were foolish.

They that were foolish took their lamps, and took no oil with them: But the wise took oil in their vessels with their lamps.

While the bridegroom tarried, they all slumbered and slept. And at midnight there was a cry made, Behold, the bridegroom cometh; go ye out to meet him.

Then all those virgins arose, and trimmed their lamps. And the foolish said unto the wise, Give us of your oil; for our lamps are gone out. But the wise answered, saying, Not so; lest there be not enough for us and you: but go ye rather to them that sell, and buy for yourselves. And while they went to buy, the bridegroom came; and they that were ready went in with him to the marriage: and the door was shut.

Afterward came also the other virgins, saying, Lord, Lord, open to us. But he answered and said, Verily I say unto you, I know you not.

Watch therefore, for ye know neither the day nor the hour wherein the Son of man cometh (Matthew 25:1-13).

We need to seek the oil of the Holy Spirit and the oil of the anointing again. We need the power of God to once again condescend to us, men and women of low estate, and fill us afresh again. We need to be equipped for this supernatural revival.

During the latter days of the Southern Kingdom, it is lamentable to think that one reformation was followed by a counter-reformation. Thus, the condition of the people was in a sad state. The prophet Jeremiah proclaimed, "The harvest is past, the summer is ended, and we are not saved" (8:20).

However, Josiah's reign proved to be a divine reprieve and one last opportunity to turn the hearts of the people of Judah back to God. At his death, Josiah was lamented greatly, as, there was no other king like Josiah, before or after him, who turned to Jehovah with all his heart, and with all his soul, and with all his might, according to all the law of Moses. (See 2 Kings 23:25.)

Could it be that the Lord's hand of judgment is only temporarily stayed from our nation now? Could it be this is our final chance to turn our hearts, families and country toward the living God? We need a formal national covenant among God's people to petition Him for a revival.

Are we ready to respond to the clarion call for revival? The prophet Hosea declared,

> Come, and let us return unto the Lord: for he hath torn, and he will heal us; he hath smitten, and he will bind us up. After two days will he revive us: in the third day he will raise us up, and we shall live in his sight. Then shall we know, if we follow on to know

the Lord: his going forth is prepared as the morning;
and he shall come unto us as the rain, as the latter
and former rain unto the earth (6:1-3).

I believe this is the third day prophetically, and though
we may have been smitten, the Lord will again raise up a
glorious church in this final hour.

Could this be the hour of revival? The Lord will not
permit us to experience revival on our terms. Rest assured we
cannot continue to ignore God's will communicated to us
through His Word and then expect the Holy Spirit's help for
the change desperately needed in our lives, homes, and
nation.

We must return to the Lord in not only word but also in
deed before our prayers for revival will be heard in heaven.
We dare not continue to challenge God's way if we want Him
to bless ours.

Let us not make a futile attempt to convince God to send
revival, while we neglect His prerequisites and continue to
break His commandments. God's Word is our road map for
this last great revival. All we need to do is what is required
therein and revival is assured.

There is a commission issued to you and me to become
the believers we always dreamed we could be—by beginning
to execute these seven keys to revival in our lives. In order to
do so, we must declare Jesus' Lordship in our personal lives,
family, country and future. We must learn to be Christ's
laborers and serve as His soldiers. We need to remember the
words of the great hymn, "Onward, Christian Soldiers."

Onward, Christian soldiers, marching as to war,
with the cross of Jesus going on before.
Christ, the royal Master, leads against the foe;
forward into battle see his banners go!

At the sign of triumph Satan's legions flee;
on then, Christian soldiers, on to victory!
Hell's foundations quiver at the shout of praise;
brothers, lift your voices, loud your anthems raise.

Like a mighty army moves the church of God;
brothers, we are treading where the saints have trod.
We are not divided, all one body we,
one in hope and doctrine, one in charity.

Crowns and thrones my perish,
kingdoms rise and wane,
but the church of Jesus constant will remain.
Gates of hell can never gainst that church prevail;
we have Christ's own promise, and that cannot fail.

Onward then, ye people, join our happy throng,
blend with ours your voices in the triumph song.
Glory, laud, and honor unto Christ the King,
this through countless ages men and angels sing.

Onward, Christian soldiers, marching as to war,
with the cross of Jesus going on before.[1]

Revival cannot come without a praying church. Revival

cannot begin without a penitent church. Revival cannot be experienced without a passionate church who is willing at all costs, like soldiers in God's army, to lay down life and limb for the higher cause of Christ.

We must refuse to allow Satan to succeed in immobilizing our commitment, incapacitating our convictions and undermining our desire to do exploits. For this race is not to the swift but to those who stand fearless and formidable in the face of defeat and—though tempted by compromise, and tried by complacency—are resolute in their relentless assault against the demon of surrender.

There will be 1,000 at your left hand and 10,000 at your right hand who will surrender to distraction, submit to defeat and succumb to the daily onslaught of the devil. They will become casualties of the crippling condition of compromise. However, true Christian soldiers are inspired by the words impossible, incurable, insurmountable and insufferable. They are soldiers who are not called great because they never fail but because they refuse to quit.

My words to you are, Onward, Christian Soldier. Though bloodied and battered, bruised and banished, we are not bowed.

I can almost hear our Commander-in-Chief, Jesus Christ, whisper to His troops, "Hold on just a little longer because the battle is almost over. Victory is assured. You shall wear a crown of righteousness."

The soul of this great nation is in our hands, and we can make a difference. Like a cool breeze, eternity is blowing around our shoulders. God is changing the times and seasons throughout America and the world.

It is time to take a personal assessment of our own lives. I believe that each of us in the body of Christ has a divine mandate to rise up and deliver the message of revival to this generation. We need to rend our hearts and not our garments and compel men, women and children to the Cross.

It is almost midnight prophetically. The groom is preparing to come back for His bride. Will we be found ready, with the souls of men and women we birthed into God's kingdom?

The prize is reserved not for those who begin but for the finishers of the race who will not be denied their position, delayed in their pursuit, or detoured on the pathway to their promise. These are they who will be counted on that grand and glorious day with those who say, "I have fought a good fight, I have finished my course, I have kept the faith: Henceforth there is laid up for me a crown of righteousness, which the Lord, the righteous judge, shall give me at that day: and not to me only, but unto all them also that love his appearing" (2 Timothy 4:7,8).

Are we ready to respond to the voice of God so that we, too, may be counted among these remnant believers? National revival cannot begin without personal revival. The decision is ours. Could it be that the choice we make will determine the course for our country and our culture?

Let us be those who cry out, "Lead on, O, King, Eternal!"

NOTES

FOREWORD
1. *Webster's New Collegiate Dictionary*, 4th. ed. (Springfield: G. & C. Merriam, Co., 1976).

2. http://www.bullatomsci.org/clock/nd95moore1.html.

CHAPTER 1
1. "Washington Gets Religion," Suzanne Fields April 9, 2001 www.washingtontimes.com/op-ed/20010409-498728.html.

2. "Foolishness to the Greeks," Lesslie Newbigin in *Christianity Today*, Vol. 30, no. 18. Bible Illustrator for Windows 3.0c, 1990-98, Parson's Technology.

3. Gordon-Conwell Theological Serminary's Founder's Day, April 4, 1989 Billy Graham in *Christianity Today*, Vol. 33, no. 9. Bible Illustrator for Windows 3.0c, 1990-98, Parson's Technology.

CHAPTER 3
1. "Ashcroft Invites God on Decisions," Larry Margasak January 11, 2001 *The Associated Press*.

2. "Ashcroft's Faith Plays Visible Role at Justice," Dan Eggen May 14, 2001 Page A01 www.washingtonpost.com/wp-dyn/articles/A23278-2001May13.html.

3. "Spiritual Awakenings in North America," *Christian History*, no. 23. Bible Illustrator for Windows 3.0c, 1990-98, Parson's Technology.

CHAPTER 4

1. "The Quotable Spurgeon," Charles Haddon Spurgeon, (Wheaton: Harold Shaw Publishers, Inc, 1990).

2. "Draper's Book of Quotations for the Christian World," Edythe Draper, (Wheaton: Tyndale House Publishers, Inc., 1992). Bible Illustrator for Windows 3.0c, 1990-98, Parson's Technology.

3. Ibid.

4. Ibid.

5. Ibid.

6. Ibid.

7. "The Quotable Spurgeon," Charles Haddon Spurgeon, (Wheaton: Harold Shaw Publishers, Inc, 1990).

8. Ibid.

CHAPTER 5

1. "The Marriage Movement: A Statement of Principles," Institute for American Values, 2000.

2. "Proposed Marriage Amendment," *The Pastor's Weekly Briefing*, 20 July 2001.

3. David Burt, "Dangerous Access 2000 Edition: Uncovering Internet Pornography in America's Libraries," Family Research Council, 2000.

4. David C. Barrett, "Annual Statistical Table on Global Missions: 2000," *International Bulletin on Missionary Research*, January 2000.

CHAPTER 6

1. Nelson's Illustrated Bible Dictionary (Nashville: Thomas Nelson Publishers, 1986). PC Study Bible for Windows 3.0c, 1993-99.

2. E.M. Bounds, "E.M. Bounds on Prayer," p. 11 (New Kensington: Whitaker House, 1997).

3. "Matthew Henry's Commentary on the Whole Bible," New Modern Edition, Electronic Database, (Nashville: Thomas Nelson Publishers, 1986). PC Study Bible for Windows 3.0c, 1993-99.

4. E.M. Bounds, "E.M. Bounds on Prayer," p. 184 (New Kensington: Whitaker House, 1997).

CHAPTER 7

1. "Nelson Illustrated Bible Dictionary," (Nashville: Thomas Nelson Publishers, 1986). PC Study Bible for Windows 3.0c, 1993-99.

2. "New Unger's Bible Dictionary," (Chicago: Moody Press, 1988). PC Study Bible for Windows 3.0c, 1993-99.

3. Louis Jennings, "The Least of These Little Ones," New York Times, 3 November 1870.

4. "Matters of Life and Death," *World*, March/April 2001, p. 16.

5. *The Pastor's Weekly Briefing*, 12 January 2001, Vol. 9, No. 2.

6. Ibid.

7. "Bush reinstates ban on international family planning funds, New administration changes balance of power on abortion issue," CNN, 22 January 2001, http://www. CNN.com/2001/ALLPOLITICS.html.

8. PR Newswire, 22 January 2001.

9. Richard John Neuhaus "Bill Clinton and the American Character," First Things, 1 June 1999.

10. Julia Duin, "Media Provide Better Coverage to Pro-Choice Side, Survey Finds," *Washington Times*, 19 January 1996, p. A8.

11. Howard Fineman, "Clinton's Values Blowout," *Newsweek*, 19 December 1994, p. 26.

12. George F. Will, "More Abortions, Fewer Crimes?," *Newsweek*, 30 April 2001, p. 84.

13. Dave Boyer, "Bush's faith-based initiative has public's blessing," *Washington Times*, 11 April 2001.

14. *Washington Times*, 31 January 2001, http://www.washingtontimes.com.html.

15. *Washington Times*, 30 January 2001, http://www.washingtontimes.com.html.

CHAPTER 10
1. "Anarchy Has Arrived," *The Pastor's Weekly Briefing*, Vo.9, No. 1727 April 2001.

2. D.L. Moody, <u>Heaven: Where It Is, Its Inhabitants, And How To Get There</u>, (Fleming H. Revell Company,1880), p. 34.

3. "Nothing but the Blood," Text: Robert Lowry, Music, Robert Lowry.

4. "At Calvary," Text: William Newell, Music: Daniel Towner.

5. "It is Well with my Soul," Text: Horatio G. Spafford, Music: Philip P. Bliss.

6. "When I Survey the Wondrous Cross," Text: Isaac Watts, Music: Lowel Mason.

7. Rupert Davies, A. Raymond George, Gordon Rupp, eds. A History of the Methodist Church in Great Britain, vol. 4 (London: Epworth Press, 1998), p. 194.

8. Spurgeon's Sermons; Charles Haddon Spurgeon, Volume 1, 1883, Baker Books, Grand Rapids, MI. p. 34.

9. Compiled by Anita Bailey, A.W. Tozer, "There is No Substitution for Theology," That Incredible Christian, (Camp Hill: Christian Publication) p. 82.

10. Peter Perl, "Absolute Truth," *The Washington Post*, 13 May 2001, p. W12.

11. Charles J. Sykes, A Nation of Victims, The Decay of American Character, (New York: St. Martin's Press 1992) p. from Prologue.

CHAPTER 11
1. Dana Mack, The Assault on Parenthood, New York: Simon & Schuster, 1997.

2. "Teens Ignorant about U.S. Independence,"
    The Pastor's Weekly Briefing, 6 July 2001, Vol. 9,
    No. 27.

3. "Senators for sound science," *World*, 30 June 2001,
    p. 8.

4. Tim Graham, "Neutral or Hostile," *World*, 2 June
    2001, p. 24.

5. Suzanne Rostler, "HIV From Heterosexual Sex Soars
    Among Teen Girls," http://www.abcnews.com,
    20 July 2001.

6. "Sex for Fun," *The Pastor's Weekly Briefing*, Vol. 9,
    No. 17, 27 April 2001.

7. Reuters, "Drug Use Rises Among Older U.S.
    Schoolkids," http://www.abcnews.com, 20 July 2001.

8. "Indoctornating Kids: NEA to Consider Resolution
    on Homosexuality," Focus on the Family Citizen
    Issues Alert, 27 June 2001, Vol. 4, No. 35.

9. Ibid.

10. "Matthew Henry's Commentary on the Whole Bible,"
    New Modern Edition, Electronic Database,
    (Nashville: Thomas Nelson Publishers, 1986).
    PC Study Bible for Windows 3.0c, 1993-99.

CHAPTER 12
1. William J. Federer, <u>American Quotations,</u> (St. Louis:
    AmeriSearch, Inc., 1996).

2.   William J. Federer, <u>America's God and Country</u>, (Coppell: FAME).

3.   William J. Federer, <u>American Quotations</u>, (St. Louis: AmeriSearch, Inc., 1996).

EPILOGUE
1.   Composed as a processional hymn for children at Horbury Bridge, near Wakefield, Yorkshire, published in *The Church Times* in 1864, and set to its now-traditional tune, "St. Gertrude," by Sir Arthur Sullivan (1842-1900) in 1871 (Handbook to the Church Hymnary, 3rd edn., ed. John M. Barkley [London: Oxford University Press, 1979], no 480, p. 174. Baring-Gould originally entitled the song "Hymn for Procession with Cross and Banners," and it is still listed among processional pieces in hymnals.

ABOUT THE AUTHOR

Rod Parsley is pastor of World Harvest Church in Columbus, Ohio, a dynamic megachurch with more than 12,000 in attendance weekly, that touches lives worldwide. He is also a highly sought-after crusade and conference speaker who delivers a life-changing message to raise the standards of physical purity, moral integrity and spiritual intensity.

Parsley also hosts *Breakthrough*, a daily and weekly television broadcast, seen by millions across America and around the world. He also oversees Bridge of Hope Missions and Outreach, World Harvest Bible College and World Harvest Christian Academy. He and his wife, Joni, have two children, Ashton and Austin.

OTHER BOOKS BY ROD PARSLEY

40 Days to Your Promised Harvest

Backside of Calvary

Breakthrough Quotes

The Commanded Blessing

Covenant Blessings

Daily Breakthrough

The Day Before Eternity

God's Answer to Insufficient Funds

He Sent His Word and Healed Them

The Jubilee Anointing

My Promise Is the Palace, So What Am I
Doing in the Pit?

No Dry Season (Best-seller)

No More Crumbs (Best-seller)

On the Brink (#1 Best-seller)

Power Through the Baptism
of the Holy Ghost

Renamed and Redeemed

Repairers of the Breach

Serious Survival Strategies

Ten Golden Keys to Your Abundance

Touched by the Anointing

Unclaimed Riches

Your Harvest is Come

For more information about Breakthrough, World Harvest
Church or to receive a product list of the many books, audio
and video tapes by Rod Parsley,
write or call:

Breakthrough
P.O. Box 32932
Columbus, Ohio 43232-0932
(614) 837-1990 (Office)

For information about World Harvest
Bible College, write or call:

World Harvest Bible College
P.O. Box 32901
Columbus, Ohio 43232-0901
(614) 837-4088

If you need prayer, Breakthrough Prayer Warriors
are ready to pray with you
24 hours a day, 7 days a week at:
(614) 837-3232

Visit Rod Parsley at his website address:
www.breakthrough.net